The Musician's Soul

Companions to *The Musician's Soul*

Audio tape library from GIA Publications:

Meditations
James Jordan
Fr. Bede Camera, OSB

The Musician's Soul:
Audio Tape Version
James Jordan

Also available by James Jordan from GIA Publications:

Evoking Sound:
Fundamentals of Choral Conducting
and Rehearsing

G-5095

The Musician's Soul

A journey examining spirituality for
performers, teachers, composers,
conductors, and music educators

James Jordan

Westminster Choir College
of Rider University

GIA Publications, Inc.
Chicago

Copyright © 1999 GIA Publications, Inc.
7404 S. Mason Ave., Chicago, IL 60638
1.800.GIA.1358 or 708.496.3800
www.giamusic.com

International Copyright Secured

ISBN: 1-57999-058-4
Printed in U.S.A.

To Elizabeth Jarrett Jordan

and

*to the Westminster Chapel Choirs of 1996, 1997, and 1998
who guided me on my journey with love and care.*

Table of Contents

Table of Contents

Lux in tenebris lucet et tenebrae eam non comprehenderunt.
(The light shines in darkness and the darkness has not understood it.)

To become conscious of anything we have first
to get the words right, because words are loaded
with implications. (p. 12)

James Hillman
Kinds of Power

This is what you shall do:
Love the earth and sun and the animals,
despise riches,
give alms to everyone that asks,
stand up for the stupid and the crazy,
devote your income and labor to others,
hate tyrants,
argue not concerning God,
have patience and indulgence toward the people,
take off your hat to nothing known or unknown or to any
    man or number of men,
go freely with powerful uneducated persons and with the
    young and with the mothers of families,
read these leaves in the open air every season of your life,
re-examine all you have been told at school or church or in
    any book,
dismiss whatever insults your own soul,
and your very flesh shall be a great poem and have the richest
    fluency
not only in its words but in the silent lines of its lips and face
and between the lashes of your eyes and in every motion and
    joint of your body.

                                                    Walt Whitman

Acknowledgments

This book has been in process for almost four years. It has ended up in a place very different from where it started. Many persons have influenced my thoughts through the classroom, reference helps, and care. To thank each and everyone is impossible, but yet, I will make a meager attempt.

My musical life has been transformed because of my exposure to mimetic theory. Donald Sheehan of Dartmouth College, whose postscript essay appears in this book, will always be the source of my deepest and most profound gratitude. He and his wife Carol have been so generous in their sharing. His willingness to help me understand mimetic theory is one of the most wonderful gifts I have ever received.

Many other persons pointed me toward books that I should read or directions that I might pursue in my thinking. Douglas Sturm, Professor Emeritus at Bucknell University, provided me with an amazing reading list that allowed me to examine soulfulness and spirituality from many different perspectives. Bede Camera, OSB, who was first a student, but has become so much more, has seen me on this journey from the very beginning. With his gentle ways and understanding, he has pointed me in the right direction, especially at times when I needed new or refreshed direction. I hope that I have also been able to teach him as he has shared and supported my work. Thanks to Kristina Groover for her help in the area of women's spirituality. Thanks to Gladys Johnson of Keene State College for her sharing of her seminal doctoral study on Martin Buber.

I have been blessed with incredible students. Many of them began as students and have become my closest friends and colleagues. Heather Buchanan, now a conductor on the Westminster faculty, came from Australia to study at Westminster. I relied on her friendship, help, encouragement, courage, insight, and honesty more than she could ever know. At the difficult times she was always there. Despite all we have been through (!), she remains one of my closest friends. Similarly, Matthew Mehaffey, came to Westminster from Bucknell University to study at Westminster. I have found his wisdom and honesty refreshing. He, too, has been in the rehearsal room constantly for over two years with me. His observations and insights have had considerable influence on me. The trust these two people placed in me to teach them is one of my greatest joys. I hope they believe likewise.

There have been many other graduate students whom it has been my honor to know and teach. Jacqueline Coren, Vincent Metallo, and Heidi Lynn all influenced this text. Gifted in their own right, each shared much with me in our time together. Craig Denison, unknowingly, had a great influence on me. Mark Kelleher, who began as Mark Kelleher, and is now Father Mark Kelleher has also made a great impact on me and my thinking throughout the years.

Special thanks to Charles Freund who took incredible care with proofing the manuscript and designing the tables. I can never thank him for all that he has done. I doubt whether this book would have been written or completed without his encouragement and care.

Thanks to Edward Harris and Alec Harris at GIA. Their belief in my work and support of this project is deeply appreciated.

Finally, the last thank you is the most difficult to express. It has been my privilege and honor to teach at the miracle that is Westminster Choir College. One simply cannot have more inspirational colleagues than the likes of Joseph Flummerfelt, Allen Crowell, Heather Buchanan, Andrew Megill, and Nancianne Parrella. Daily, I stand in front of what must be one of the most remarkable ensembles of first-year students anywhere in the world. They, perhaps better than anyone, have experienced my journey and know of my commitment to it. The music we make has pointed the way for me in all of this. Their trust in me can never be repaid. Their care and love has taught me much.

I am sure that I have not mentioned many people who have had an influence on this book and my ideas. There are simply too many. While they are not mentioned, they are not forgotten. I am humbled by all of you who have helped me. May each of you be pleased with this work.

— James Jordan
Princeton
May, 1999

Part One

SETTING THE STAGE

Chapter One
Introduction

To go to the source, especially in America, calls for a new heartfelt appreciation of ideas in and for themselves. Perhaps ideas are the single most precious miracle in human existence. For ideas determine our goals of action, our styles of art, our values of character, our religious practices and even our ways of loving. (p. 16)

James Hillman
Kinds of Power

It takes courage to grow up and turn out to be who you really are. (p. 43)

e. e. cummings in
John Fox, *Finding What You Didn't Lose*

It is very difficult to elucidate the (cosmic religious) feeling to anyone who is entirely without it....The religious geniuses of all ages have been distinguished by this kind of religious feeling, which knows no dogma....In my view, it is the most important function of art and science to awaken this feeling and keep it alive in those who are receptive to it. (p. 174)

Albert Einstein in
V. S. Ramachandran and Sandra Blakeslee,
Phantoms in the Brain

Nothing is better than music. When it takes us out of time, it has done more for us than we have the right to hope for. It has broadened the limits of our sorrowful lives; it has lit up the sweetness of our hours of happiness by effacing the pettinesses that diminish us, bringing us back pure and new to what was, what will be and what music has created for us. (p. 63)

Those men who have lit up the road for eternity were always alone in the midst of the multitude, alone among loved ones, alone in seeing too high, too far, alone in some terrifying solitude, because the questions that reared up between them and the unknown are scarcely conceivable to us. (p. 61)

Nadia Boulanger in
Don G. Campbell, *Master Teacher*

With all your science can you tell how it is, and whence it is that light comes into the soul?

Henry David Thoreau
Walden, 1854

One must still have chaos in oneself to be able to give birth to a dancing star.

Friederich Nietzche

No pessimist ever discovered the secrets of the stars, or sailed to an uncharted land, or opened a new heaven to the human spirit. (p. xxi)

Helen Keller in
Mark Bryan, *The Artist's Way at Work*

Human understanding is like an irregular mirror, which distorts and discolors the nature of things by mingling its own nature with it. (p. 15)

Francis Bacon
Novum Organum

Are there then no traits that distinguish creative people? If I had to express in one word what makes their personalities different from others, it would be complexity. By this I mean that they show tendencies of thought and action that in most people are segregated. They contain contradictory extremes—instead of being an "individual," each of them is a "multitude." Like the color white that includes all hues of the spectrum, they tend to bring together the entire range of human possibilities within themselves. (p. 57)

Mihaly Csikszentmihalyi
Creativity

The soul of the human species is sometimes called the collective unconscious, but it is not that. It is the soul of human kind. Your soul is a miniature of the soul of the human species. It is a micro of a macro. It has as much energy and power. As part of the micro, you have all the power of the macro calibrated to the individual form of certain frequencies. You form collective energies that help the whole evolve, although they are not themselves souls, and do not have souls. In between the macro and the micro are the various experiences afforded the individual human soul learning within a group, participating in group evolution, such as the evolution of your country, your religion, and the individual personal experiences that comprise the human experience. (p. 117)

Gary Zukav
The Seat of the Soul

Teaching, like any truly human activity, emerges from one's inwardness, for better or worse. As I teach, I project the condition of my soul onto my students, my subject, and our way of being together. The entanglements I experience in the classroom are often no more or less than the convolutions of my inner life. Viewed from this angle, teaching holds a mirror to the soul. If I am willing to look in that mirror and not run from what I see, I have a chance to gain self-knowledge—and knowing myself is as crucial to good teaching as knowing my students and my subject.

In fact, knowing my students and my subject depends heavily on self-knowledge. When I do not know myself, I cannot know who my students are. I will see them through a glass darkly, in the shadows of my unexamined life—and when I cannot see them clearly I cannot teach them well. When I do not know myself, I cannot know my subject—not at the deepest levels of embodied, personal meaning. I will know it only abstractly, from a distance, a congeries of concepts as far removed from the world as I am from personal truth. (p.2)

Parker J. Palmer
The Courage to Teach

It helps, I think, to consider ourselves on a very long journey: the main thing is to keep to the path, to endure, to help each other when we stumble or tire, to weep and press on. Perhaps if I had a coat of arms, this would be my motto: Weep and begin again. (p. 140)

M. C. Richards
Centering: In Pottery, Poetry, and the Person

This book will not provide you with many definitive answers regarding music making. This book is written by a musician whose primary performance medium is conducting. Many will assume, mistakenly so, that it is a handbook of conducting. While the book is written from the viewpoint of a conductor, that viewpoint can be applied to any means of sharing music, whether it be ensemble performance or teaching. When working with groups of persons making music, it is important to recognize that human beings involved in the creative act bring to bear upon that music making their entire humanity, the experience of their lives. If there is a person who stands at the front of that group of persons, then the humanity of that person is an important catalyst in the dynamic of musical creation.

This book will attempt to "point the way" and provide insights into the inside stuff of conducting. The risks of oversimplification of a complex human state are great. I do not claim to have the answers; in fact I am not sure I have any answers. Our life issues, which bear symbiotically and directly on the music being sounded, are both different and diverse. I am fairly certain, however, of the direction that this journey should take. I would also like to convince you that if you desire the highest level of music making from your classes and ensembles, you must take the journey; you must walk the walk. For each of us, the route of the journey will be different, but our direction must be the same. The route of your personal journey is determined, for the most part, by your life experiences. There must be an honesty within yourself that will allow you to trust yourself to make the journey to seek experiences that will provide answers and possibly new directions.

It has been said that books are usually about one thing. It has also been said that life is about one thing. The journey of this book is about one idea: you must trust, believe, and love yourself. Music making is constructed of correct notes, correct rhythms, dynamics, and articulation. But the mortar of music is human trust (of self and others), belief in self and others, and love of self.

Love of self is immediately magnified through music to love of others. This book will ask you to explore, find, and know the deepest parts of your being and to bring that newfound depth to all that you do musically. To be open to any possibility is a living definition of soulfulness.

This book is about that direction and possibility.

I do not claim to have answers, for I, too, am on this journey. After twenty years of conducting and teaching, and almost as many years teaching the strange art form of conducting to hundreds of students, I have come to some realizations. Many of them seem obvious now, but were very difficult to come by. I expect that if you speak to me in twenty years hence, some of those realizations will be the same, some will be different. I do know that all those realizations will be the products of my own life experiences with choirs and great music. But most importantly, they will always be about experiences with and between people, tempered by thinking, reasoning, arguing, and questioning within myself mixed with a good dose of intuition born out of making music with others.

As I observe the conducting profession, specifically the choral music genre, I have seen many fine teachers and "conductors." Their choirs sing beautifully with impeccable intonation. I have taught many conducting students who possess technical conducting gifts; that is, their hands work well. Coordination and symmetry of pattern is seemingly effortless. Yet, whether it be a children's choir or an adult professional chorus, many times there is something missing in the sound: that something which provides a brilliance of color and accuracy of pitch that is unmistakable, if one is listening. What is missing? What is missing to those who really listen is a humanness to the sound. A sound that is born because of the conductor's selflessness and understanding of human love through music. The often used expression "the music has no soul" is not far from the truth and the aural reality.

I have great concerns for music education. At the risk of overgeneralizing, music education has understandably focused itself on techniques of teaching, and sometimes on the methods of teaching and its consequent learning. However, the profession has not remained focused on those basic, bottom-line elements which allow children and adults to make music that really have little, if anything, to do with the reading and replication of the right pitch and right rhythm. Music in the classroom and ensembles can be "made," but it is created and generated from the very souls of those that produce it. Soulful human beings create profound music, regardless of their level of musical achievement. Such music is, at the same time, honest and direct, and speaks in the most direct way to all that hear it.

The pedagogy of conducting has likewise focused on the teaching of technique. In many quarters, it has focused on a teaching of conducting devoid of sound. The author made an attempt to approach that problem in the book *Evoking Sound* (1996). This book will not revisit materials in that book, but will use one of the major points of that book as a point of departure. A conductor does not "conduct;" he, by the nature of his being and his spirit, causes people to sing; he evokes sounds that hopefully, are reflective of each person's individual life experiences. Granted, technique and the mechanics of conducting must be taught and respected. However, the stuff that allows for the creation of great music is rarely dealt with in the teaching of conducting. What is usually easiest learned is hardest taught. Soulfulness is a hard thing to talk about and teach.

Self-Expression and Center

If one believes that music is self-expression, then it should follow that one must have a self to express. Before one is able to conduct and evoke artistry from singers, one must spend a considerable amount of time on oneself, on one's inside stuff. One must take time to understand and accept who one is. One must learn how to trust oneself at all times. Most musicians, however, involve themselves in a process of self-mutilation. They focus on the "why" and "how" of music instead of the "who." Frustration and anger with self occur, almost unknowingly. The conductor, music educator, or performer must spend a considerable amount of time with him- or herself to make the journey that will deepen understanding of self and of his or her own human spirit. That journey must be non–self-mutilating. At the risk of oversimplifying, one must be able to love oneself first before that love can be shared with an ensemble or an audience through the music. Knowledge and trust of self is necessary for music making to take place. An ability to "just be" is paramount.

In order to share oneself honestly with the singers, one must also have a center around which one's being holds forth. The word "center" is synonymous with many things, all of which form the core of a life and a person. A person's commitment to life, his awareness of the world around him, and his understanding of the beauty of the world and his own life are the foundation of a musician's center. It is out of this center that human impulse is channeled which, in turn, influences the pulse, musical line, and the color of the textures in the composer's world. Great composers compose music from their unique centers. But make no mistake about it, the conducting and creation of music flows from this thing called center. Center is the total integration of life and soul; inner being and outer being become one.

The Order of the Journey

This book can be read from the beginning to the end as the chapters have been arranged by the author. However, some chapters may have more relevance to your life than others. The chapters that you determine as not relevant should be considered only as such if you can honestly answer that you have made the journey suggested in that chapter. If you believe that a chapter is

unimportant, it may be that it is that very chapter which contains
your most serious issue or issues. In such a case, I would ask you
to take a deep breath and examine yourself again. I have found
that many students would not consider a certain chapter because
it either frightened them to go to the place that was suggested, or
they found it difficult to journey to the place suggested because of
something that has occurred in their lives that prevented access. I
would encourage each of you to take all of the journeys
suggested...again and again. You should visit those places daily. I
know that these places, once inhabited, will transform your music
making forever. Only after blending all the information in these
chapters can we attempt to describe the musician's soul. One
could consider this book a collection of ideas, words, and experiences on how to chart a journey to understand oneself more. In
this book, Center and Soul are synonymous. One's center is one's
soul, and vice versa.

This book is by no means complete. The journeys and how I
have thought about them vary. The way I have taken the journeys
vary with my experience. You vicariously cannot have my experiences; you must substitute your own experiences that are parallel
in order for my words to resonate. Some chapters are the result of
journeys that I have taken. Many of the journeys were led by the
great teachers in my life. Some of the journeys were led by the
choirs that I have conducted. Those journeys led by choirs happened almost by accident; it was the power of their spirits and
their selflessness when singing that caused me to travel with them
because of our love for the music. Some of the journeys were led
by great composers through their music. Some have been the by-
products of the conducting classroom. Some were the product of
my experiences as an instrumental performer. All journeys, in
whole or in part, are always the result of an acquired ability to
quiet my self-clatter to try to hear my own unique voice.

Throughout the book, I will constantly change the perspective
from which I address an issue: sometimes I will address issues as a

conductor, sometimes I will address issues from the perspective of a singer, and at other times I will use the umbrella term "musician." The simple fact of the matter is that despite the performance medium and regardless of whether one deals with a choral ensemble, an audience, or an orchestra, the soulful issues about music making are always the same. I also believe that this material is relevant to journeys outside the discipline of music. I hope not to confuse you with the shifting perspectives, but I think those shifting perspectives are important to gain a universal, overall view of the challenges involved.

This book also contains meditations on cassette tape which is a required companion to this book. The written chapters, hopefully, will give you ideas, words, and experiences that will help to bring you to an understanding of Center and Soul. The meditations are a valuable aspect of the book in that they provide you with a vehicle on and in which to take your journey. I know that while they are valuable for conductors and teachers, they are equally valuable for ensembles. That, however, is the subject matter for another time and place. I will say that if you are able to take some of the journeys yourself, you will want to take your ensembles on the same journeys. If you do, their music making will approach new heights.

For those of you who are familiar with *Evoking Sound*, you will again see quotes that either serve to deepen the meaning of the chapter they precede, or provide further material for thought and examination. I wanted to share with you ideas and words that I have found inspirational and many times speak much better than I to the particular point at hand. The quotes in this text, as in *Evoking Sound*, could and should form a text of their own for future study.

I mentioned earlier that this book is about ideas, ideas that are rooted in experiences. The problem that I confront in this text is the danger of oversimplicity. Einstein has been paraphrased to have said, "Everything should be as simple as it can be, but not overly simple." I have attempted to relate the experiences and ideas that I believe both through my experience and the experience of others will lead one in the direction of soulfulness in a simple and direct way. I hope that in my attempt to do so I did not oversimplify or trivialize the profoundness of the experience.

Beginning to Understand: The Nature of the Creative Being

I think some time must be spent understanding the complex nature of those who are involved in creative activities. Thomas Moore, in his book *Care of the Soul,* makes a strong point that all human beings are complex. He also makes the point that when one is attempting to deal with the problems of one's life, it is foolhardy to believe that one's problems will disappear. He instead advocates keeping them in the proper perspective.

If the general description of the human state is as complex as Moore describes it, then what is the state of the creative artist? Mihaly Csikszentmihalyi in his book *Creativity* (1996, pp. 57-76) details those characteristics that he has found in creative individuals. They are listed below:

1. Creative individuals have a great deal of physical energy, but they are often quiet and at rest.
2. Creative individuals tend to be smart, yet also naive at the same time.
3. A third paradoxical trait refers to the related combination of playfulness and discipline, or responsibility and irresponsibility.
4. Creative individuals alternate between imagination and fantasy at one end, and a rooted sense of reality at the other.
5. Creative people seem to harbor opposite tendencies on the continuum between extroversion and introversion.

6. Creative individuals are also remarkably humble and proud at the same time.

7. In all cultures, men are brought up to be the "masculine" and to disregard and repress those aspects of their temperament that the culture regards as "feminine," whereas women are expected to do the opposite.

8. Generally, creative people are thought to be rebellious and independent.

9. Most creative persons are very *passionate* about their work, yet they can be extremely *objective* about it as well.

10. Finally, the openness and sensitivity of creative individuals often exposes them to *suffering and pain yet also a great deal of enjoyment.*

I list the above points for several reasons. First, many musicians that I teach, whether they are in choirs or in conducting classes, believe themselves to be an oddity. They believe that they are inherently unstable. They are the only ones who have so many issues. Many of them have never understood their bouts with either minor or major depressive patterns. If they have sought help from a professional via counseling, the counselor generally treats them as any other person, not recognizing the additional complexities they bring to the table because they are artists. Many of these persons, I find, believe themselves to be abnormal with abnormal problems and abnormal feelings. I remember the comment of one of my music therapy professors in graduate school. He always referred to the population labeled in the textbooks as "abnormal" as the "normal" population. His point was that there is no such condition as "normal." After the passage of time and much experience, I tend to agree with him.

The above list should not be used as an excuse for bizarre, out-of-the-mainstream behavior—"I am entitled to do this, I am an artist." This perceptive list is provided to place your fears at ease and to give you some maneuvering space, so that you can begin to understand yourself. In a future chapter, I label the above list as an artistic curse. In many ways, it is. Along with the ability to create beauty comes another entire set of emotional and psychological challenges. These, however, are the positives. They are the things which make our lives rich and colorful and provide us with the gifts that allow us, ultimately, to listen to our own creative voices.

One last thought. If you choose to explore any of the areas in these chapters, one of the new issues that you will confront is a heightened state of awareness of the world around you, and, at times, a painfully acute awareness of yourself. At times this aware-ness is a curse of sorts because you are constantly thinking and reacting as a result of that new-found awareness. Many times you will want to "shut it off." As I discuss later in the book, awareness is a necessary condition for the artist in the world. Without aware-ness, there can be no growth, little honest music, and little love. Great music is made in a state of awareness. Be challenged by the ideas that follow, and follow the callings they issue to you.

Chapter Two
"Give Me Some Old Time Religion"

It goes without saying that spiritual writing is not about
God. It is about the human longing for all that God can
mean. It may be possible to be an atheist, but it is probably impossible, once alive, not to respond to the presence of something—soul, spirit, lifeforce, you name it—
that the human core from which the cry of anguish and
the whoop of joy emanate. The sheer instinct to record
these experiences of extremity is, in itself, a spiritual act.
(p. xxiii)

> Patricia Hampl in
> Philip Zaleski, *Spiritual Writing*

It is customary to blame secular science and anti-reli-
gious philosophy for the eclipse of religion in modern
society. It would be more honest to blame religion for its
own defeats. Religion declined not because it refuted, but
because it became irrelevant, dull, oppressive, insipid.
When faith is completely replaced by creed, worship by
discipline, love by habit; when the crisis of today is
ignored because of the splendor of the past; when faith
becomes an heirloom rather than a living fountain; when
religion speaks only in the name of authority rather than
with the voice of compassion, its message becomes
meaningless. (p. 35)

As civilization advances, the sense of wonder declines. Such decline is an alarming symptom of our state of mind. Mankind will not perish for want of information, but only for want of appreciation. The beginning of our happiness lies in the understanding that life without wonder is not worth living. What we lack is not a will to believe, but a will to wonder. (p. 41)

The sense for the "miracles which are daily with us," the sense for the "continual marvels," is the source of prayer. There is no worship, no music, no love, if we take for granted the blessings or defeats of living....This is one of the goals of the Jewish way of living: to experience commonplace deeds as spiritual adventures, to feel hidden love and wisdom in all things. (p. 43)

The sense of the ineffable, the awareness of the grandeur and mystery of living, is shared by all men, and it is in the depth of such awareness that acts and thoughts of religion are full of meaning. (p. 48)

Abraham Joshua Heschel
Between God and Man

In labor, when a Shaker focuses her or his mind on the here and now, any chore becomes a chance to serve God and community. Any task becomes meaningful, beautiful, worth the effort. Devotion infuses pies, ordinary as they look, shaped by Sister Marie. Meditation pulls together yarns of rich earth colors on Brother Arnold's loom. Prayer seeps between the lines of a column written by Sister Frances for the Shaker newsletter. Hope smooths soft blankets knit for unknown babies by Sister Ruth's gnarled hands. Praise lifts the hoe of Brother Wayne high into the air for hour after sweaty hour of repetitive motion. Joy lights the library as Sister June hunches over another pile of catalog cards to be carefully

sorted for researchers' use. And serenity floods the
sewing workshop where Brother Alistair sorts through a
cardboard box of fabric scraps to plan his next craft for
the Christmas fair. Buddhists call this mindfulness.
Managers call this focus. Shakers call this practice their
most important motto: "Put your hands to work and
your hearts to God." (p. 168)

Suzanne Skees
God Among the Shakers

Spirituality means waking up. Most people, even though
they don't know it, are asleep. They're born asleep, they
live asleep, they marry in their sleep, they breed children
in their sleep, they die in their sleep without ever waking
up. They never understand the loveliness and the beauty
of this thing that we call human existence. You know, all
mystics—Catholics, Christian, non-Christian, no matter
what their theology, and no matter what their religion—
are unanimous on one thing that all is well, that all is well.
Though everything is a mess, all is well. Strange paradox
to be sure, but tragically, most people never get to see
that all is well because they are asleep. They are having a
nightmare. (p. 5)

Spirituality is the most practical thing in the whole wide
world. I challenge anyone to think of anything more practical than spirituality as I have defined it—not piety, not
devotion, not religion, not worship, but spirituality—waking up—waking up! Look at the heartache everywhere,
look at the loneliness, look at the fear, the confusion, the
conflicts in the hearts of people, inner conflict, outer conflict. Suppose somebody gave you a way of getting rid of
all of that? Suppose somebody gave you a way to stop
the tremendous drainage of energy, of health, of emotion
that comes from these conflicts and confusion. Would
you want that? Suppose someone showed us a way
whereby we would truly love one another, and be at

peace, be at love. Can you think of anything more practical than that? But that politics is more practical. What's the earthly use of putting a man on the moon when we cannot live on the earth? (p. 11)

Anthony deMello
Awareness

There are two, and in the end only two, types of faith. To be sure there are many contents of faith, but we only know faith in two basic forms. Both can be understood from the simple data of our life; the one from the fact that I trust someone, without being able to offer sufficient reasons for my trust in him; the other from the fact that, likewise without being able to give sufficient reason, I acknowledge a thing to be true. In both cases my not being able to give a sufficient reason is not a matter of a defectiveness in my ability to think, but of a real peculiarity in my relationship to the one whom I trust or that which I acknowledge to be true. It is a relationship which by its nature does not rest upon "reasons," just as it does not grow from such; reasons of course can be urged for it, but they are never sufficient to account for my faith. (p. 7)

My rationality, my rational power of thought, is merely a part, a particular function of my nature; when however I "believe," in either sense, my entire being is engaged, the totality of my nature enters into the process, indeed this becomes possible only because the relationship of faith is a relationship of my entire being. (p. 8)

The relationship of trust depends on a state of contact, a contact of my entire being with the one whom I trust, the relationship of acknowledging depends on an act of acceptance by my entire being which I acknowledge to be true. (p. 8)

Martin Buber
Two Types of Faith

In order not to start us all off on some bad footing, the problem, or rather the definition of religion, a.k.a. "spirituality," needs to be discussed. Uneasiness may start to overtake many reading this far in this text. It is that type of uneasiness that sometimes results when ideas about "religion" are thrust upon one in a conversation. Spirituality, depending upon which generation one is a member, likewise may hearken uncomfortable, if not unsettling, images. For those of us who have ignored this aspect of our lives, the subject may be, well, simply uncomfortable and unsettling. All of these feelings and thoughts are filtered through the various colored prisms of our own religiosity or lack thereof.

All of us carry within us a set of religious ideas that have been nurtured in some way in our lives. This part of our life is, indeed, important, but it does not form the core of who we are spiritually as human beings. In fact, some of our difficulties in making music with others may lie in the fact that we have extreme difficulty moving beyond personal religious dogma to the larger spiritual picture that music forces us to consider. That is not to say that one's personal religious "genetics" should be dismissed out of hand. As artists, however, we are entrusted with the responsibility, I believe, to probe deeper into our own spiritual selves using a number of inroads. For some it may be through Yoga. For others, it may be through meditation. For some it will be through reading religious scripture from the viewpoint of an artist. For others it may be through poetry. Eastern philosophies may unlock doors for some that have been closed for most of their lives. Tai Chi may be yet another vehicle.

What is common to all of the above is that they each, in their own way, provide time for quiet and stillness in one's crazy, busy life. One's innermost spiritual seat, the place from which all musical impulse grows and is nourished, can only be accessed through time spent with one's self. Time for reflection. Time for listening to one's inner voice, which, when heard, speaks ultimate truth which is then reflected in music. Yes, this book is advocating some type of spiritual centering in one's life as a prerequisite to music making. But in the larger world sense, the book is also advocating spirituality in order to develop humanness within oneself, and an understanding of what love is. Not necessarily love of others, but, first and foremost, the love of oneself. If one can love oneself, one also respects oneself and begins to understand what it is to just "be." Just "being" is one of the most difficult tasks that we all have in this increasingly complicated world. How can we begin to see the truth among us amidst all of the complication if we do not have the ability to calm ourselves and look inward for some fundamental truths?

I believe that within every artist is contained, deep within the "soul," a fundamental set of truths; without it, he or she would probably not be an artist. I do believe that persons who do not practice artistic expression have them, too, but they continually slip away if not used. Hence the reason why people sing and play and have a basic love for music and the arts. Innate sensibilities about beauty and the fundamental profundities of life: birth, re-birth, struggle, separation, trust, compassion, hope and the contemplation of the end of one's life, death. To quote the old hymn, "Give me some old time religion."

Is It Religion or Is It Faith?

Perhaps, however, one of the problems for the artist, or for anyone for that matter, is that the lines that distinguish faith from religion become blurred. They become blurred, perhaps, due to an unawareness of the difference between the two. The quote from the old hymn tune "Give me some old time religion" would better be stated as "Give me some old time faith."

One's religion is how one chooses to practice one's faith. It is one's faith which forms and fosters the soul's interiority and depth. Faith in each one of us is omnipresent if we will make ourselves aware that it is within us. Our faith is our spirituality. The human condition, with all of its difficulties, does have at its core a spirituality that lives within each of us. It is the quest for understanding that spirituality within each of us that we cannot deny if we are to grow as artists and musicians. How one chooses to explore and practice one's spirituality is a matter of choice. Many conductors I have taught and observed practice their religion or religious choices in front of their ensemble. If they are Catholic, they speak of Catholicism. Fundamentalist Christians may overlay their religious teachings onto every piece of music that they conduct. The fact that one practices their faith as a Catholic, Fundamentalist Christian, Jew, or Buddhist is a matter of choice. What one brings to one's artistic life is one's faith, or more directly put, one's spirituality. If one examines the lives of Bach, Britten, Brahms, Mendelssohn, Stravinsky, Vaughan Williams, and Ives, one can study how they chose to practice their faith. However, if one listens to their music, one hears their faith and their spirituality, never their religion. In order for that composer's voice to speak, a kindred spirit must be operating as the performer and interpreter of that music: one who is on a quest of awareness and one who brings one's faith to interact with that of the composers. I believe that composers' and other artistic creators' faith speaks through their music. Their faith is universal and speaks to all who listen with the tools of their own faith, but not through the colored glasses of their own religion. Religion is how one chooses to practice one's faith. Religion, which is born of man, is inherently flawed because it does reflect at times the frailties of the life situation. Religion is one important vehicle in the journey of faith. It is not the only vehicle, however. The door to one's faith is an awareness that is fostered by quiet time to hear one's faith. Time for solitude. Time for quiet. Time for reflection. Time for understanding of self. And the ability to accept the quiet time as a fundamental privilege of life. Understanding and experiencing one's own faith and enormous interiority can only be understood and explored through time with oneself on a daily basis.

Faith Brought to Music: Wonder and Awe

So, it probably is not the old time religion that we are after here, although some may believe that. What we are after is an awareness of faith realized through a newly discovered sense of interiority, a renewed sense of personal spirituality, and a renewed sense of soulful spaciousness that becomes our new home for making music. We need a chance again to be with ourselves so that we learn to know and recognize our spiritual and soulful instincts. Many of us will discover them again as old friends. Still many others may meet them for the first time. And yet others will endure a painful struggle to make the journey.

Choirs do not sing as well or honestly and orchestras do not play as well or honestly when the person who is standing in front of them avoids, usually unknowingly, being in touch with these "life" or "spiritual" truths. All of those life truths can be summarized in the weak semantics of the words "care" and "love." I have heard it said that "God" is not a noun, but rather is a verb. The God for each of us that brings meaning to our life grows out of our own stillness. The "God" that is a verb in all the music we make. That perhaps is closer to the journey we each need to take if we love our art, and those who create our art with us. To be able to also be aware of the grandeur and sublime in our lives, to be able to sense that "miracles are with us on a daily basis." As Abraham Joshua Heschel additionally points out in the quote that begins this chapter, what we lack is not a will to believe, but a will to wonder. It is that sense of wonder that is born out of one's "soulfullness" accessed through stillness that infuses our music with honesty and life messages that reflect soulful faith.

I am beginning to think that such is the stuff of an artistic life well lived. I do sense that if we begin to make these journeys and continue to make them, that our music will move from something we apprehend to something we truly and deeply comprehend. If choirs are taught to sing from the origin of their own spirituality, then composers will be given the voice that they truly deserve.

Part Two

EXPLORING SOULFULNESS

Chapter Three

Three Important Ingredients: Being Open, Being Vulnerable, and Knowing Your Center

Everyone thinks of changing the world, but no one thinks of changing himself. (p. 160)

Leo Tolstoy in
Mark Bryan, *The Artist's Way at Work*

When I talk with some of my psychiatrist friends and some of my psychologist friends and some of my medical and clerical friends, and even with the few legal friends that I have, and we get down to cases, we discover that the basic fundamental thing that appears to hold our professional lives together and define all our relationships with our clients and our parishioners and our colleagues is not sin, which you might expect me to say, but fear. Everybody is fearful, terrified of some public or private demon, some terrible unnamed fear that gnaws away even in the midst of our joy, some cloud that hangs over our head or in the recesses of our spirit. It is fear that not only holds us together but keeps us from being whole. Fear, not sin, is the great curse. Fear that I'll be recognized for the fraud that I am—the great imposter complex. Fear that I will fail in some worthy endeavor or

fear that I will succeed in some unworthy enterprise. Fear
that I will not have enough time to do what I must. Fear
that I will hurt or be hurt. Fear that I will not know love.
Fear that my love will be painful and hurtful. Fear that the
things that I most believe and trust are not so. Fear that I
am untrustworthy. Everyone of us is hostage to fear.
(p. 77)

Peter J. Gomes
Sermons

Our problems are inside our lives, yes; but our lives are
lived inside fields of power, under the influence of others,
in accordance with authority, subject to tyrannies.
Moreover, our lives are lived inside fields of power that
are our cities with their offices and cars, systems of work
and mountains of trash. These too are powers impinging
in our souls. When the wider world breaks down and is
sick at heart, the individual suffers accordingly. (p. 15)

James Hillman
Kinds of Power

It is better to confess that virtually nothing happens for
which we are not ourselves more or less directly responsible. We should look for our part of the blame in each
event. (p. 78)

We are often mistaken about art. Art is not emotion.
Art is the medium in which emotion is expressed. (p. 77)

Your mind does not listen, but your heart will remember. (p. 71)

You are all deep. It is the deepness of you I want to
meet within me. This may bore you, but I do not care
because some year you will remember, somehow. (p. 70)

Nadia Boulanger in
Don G. Campbell, *Master Teacher*

Allow yourself to become aware of what you feel. Give yourself permission to choose the most positive behavior in each moment. As you discharge negative energy consciously and set your intentions according to what your heart tells you, as you challenge and release your fears and choose to heal, you align your personality with your soul and move toward becoming a being of Light, fully whole and empowered and inwardly secure. Humbleness, forgiveness, charity and love, all gifts of the spirit, take root and bloom, and you draw to yourself the Universe's greatest gift: human beings with open hearts. (p. 248)

Gary Zukav
The Seat of the Soul

Contemporary philosophers frequently connect consciousness with virtue, and although they constantly talk of freedom they rarely talk of love. (p. 2)

Prayer is properly not petition, but simply an attention to God, which is a form of love. (p. 55)

Iris Murdoch
The Sovereignty of Good

To be able to make music, one should make a presupposition. That presupposition is that one is able to be open and vulnerable to the ensemble. Being able to open oneself to the ensemble, to the audience or to the classroom makes an assumption that one can be open to oneself and vulnerable to the world at large. That is, the musician has the ability to be himself devoid of ego, and that he is able to travel to the place within himself where all impulses for making music live. One can only access that place through quietness and calm. It can be said that music is created out of the quiet, centered self. For most of us, accessing center through quietness will be our most formidable challenge.

What is the definition of openness? This is indeed a difficult question. Openness is the ability to recognize, accept, and trust oneself; to understand and appreciate the experiences that contribute to one's life. To be able to find a place deep within oneself that is at peace and calm out of which life's experiences and one's music are quietly reflected. It is that reflection, then, that a choir, an ensemble, or a classroom uses as a vehicle into a musical experience. Trust of oneself and profound human trust that is rooted in the most basic human love is the core of all musical experience and interaction. In order to make music, one must be able to meet others on the equal ground of trusting and loving. In order to accomplish that goal, one must be able to look inward and realize the trust and love that already exists within oneself. This is not an easy task, because the mistrust engendered by the world around us has constructed an almost impermeable protective shell. This shell is impermeable to those outside, and in many ways hides us from ourselves. The shell thickens and hardens as we look for answers outside of ourselves instead of listening to ourselves. The shell further calcifies when we do not spend enough time to understand, love, and respect ourselves.

Vulnerability

This term I find used with increasing regularity not only in music, but in other disciplines. The term is used frequently as a semantic umbrella that brings with it great mystery and a certain degree of awe to those upon whom it is thrust. Musicians are told that they must be vulnerable if their music is to be honest. Conducting students are told that they must be more vulnerable and work "harder" to open themselves in front of the ensemble. "Be vulnerable." "You are not vulnerable enough when you conduct." "I do not hear vulnerability in the sound of the choir."

The use of the vulnerability label is easy. But as the expression goes, what is usually easiest learned is hardest taught. And so it goes with the subject of vulnerability. Let there be no doubt, however, that one's ability to be vulnerable and become vulnerable is a necessary component of music making. One's vulnerability allows another to experience a spirit and to engage a living soul through music. A more important component of an artistic relationship simply does not exist.

I have found that I cannot describe vulnerability. I have also discovered that I cannot teach it. Vulnerability is born out of each person's unique experience, hence it defies description. One can only define vulnerability through one's own life experience. I believe that every human being has experienced vulnerability in some aspect of his life. But the key to understanding vulnerability is experience. You must either directly experience an event that will cause you to be vulnerable or you must know someone with whom you interact on a regular basis who exhibits vulnerability. The real challenge is to recall that experience or experiences in life when you were vulnerable, and travel to that place deep within you whenever you conduct or make music.

Vulnerability Taught by Life

My tutorial in vulnerability occurred later in my development, unfortunately, at the age of thirty-nine. To paraphrase Carolyn Chute on the subject of her autobiography, the subject has been involuntarily researched by the author. While I would gladly trade the event for anything else, and would much rather that it did not occur, occur it did.

On December 28, 1991 at approximately 6:15 in the evening, I arrived home after completing some errands. My wife and daughter were waiting at the door for me. Their faces told most of the story. My wife told me to call my mother. I picked up the phone and dialed. The phone did not complete one ring, and mom answered. I immediately asked a one-word question, "Mom?" "Your dad is gone. He came home from work tonight, sat down to eat dinner, looked at me, and died. I knew he was gone, almost instantly. I tried everything, but there was nothing I could do, except tell him I loved him." I said nothing. There was a halting silence. "Don't come home tonight, there is nothing you can do tonight. Friends are here to look after me." Amidst lots of tears, I told my Mom how much I loved her and hung up the phone.

I remember getting off the phone, being totally unable to speak. Bewildered. I also remember vividly this vacant, expansive, yet totally helpless feeling. It was as if someone pulled a stopper and all my emotional "stuff" was emptied from my body. I loved my dad. I don't think he ever really fully realized how much, because as I was growing up, I never spoke about my feelings. I lived with them, but never seemed able to verbalize them. But love him I did. One of the most important persons in my daughter's life, her granddad, was gone. She still speaks of him with so much love to this day.

Dad's funeral, like all funerals, was a bit surreal. I was deeply touched by the fact that two of my best high school friends who I had not seen in well over twenty years were there. When I asked them in amazement why they had traveled so far, their reply was simply, "to be here for you and your Mom." I was taken aback by their care. That seemed to offset the pain that my closest friend didn't show or even call.

As literally hundreds of persons showed up at the viewing one hour before the burial on New Year's Eve, my entire life before age eighteen passed in front of me. Age eighteen for most of us marks passage into the adult world, away from home—college and life. But what struck me that day is that all these people from my life were forgotten by me. It was almost as if in my "hunt" for my career, they were the cast-offs. People from my father's garage that I knew since I was four. The widow of our family physician whose husband raised a sickly little boy and treated him as one of his own. All of a sudden it struck me. This is who I am that I have lost sight of. Like it or not, despite my position at Westminster

Choir College, I was Jim Jordan from Frackville, Pennsylvania. How could I wipe all this out of my memory? I thought. What causes us to do this?

I stayed with my mother for several weeks, and then returned to Westminster. I can remember being afraid of the first rehearsal with the choir. I had never been afraid of a rehearsal before. What makes this one so different? I thought. Soon I would find out.

I entered that rehearsal room at one o'clock like I had done for almost two years. Yet, there was something very different about this day. I looked at the choir first, and then spoke. I do not remember what I said. It is not important now. I can remember doing a familiar piece from the Christmas program. I was in a state of shock. I *heard* the piece, I realized, for the first time. I was also able to breathe (a problem that I had been grappling with for years). And the choir sounded very different.

Rehearsals became a joy, and tour that year ended with some beautiful music making. One of the students asked me, after the tour was over, "What happened to you? We are singing so differently than we did in the beginning of the year."

I wish my Dad were still here. But, in all honesty, the first time I ever allowed myself to be vulnerable, or was made to be vulnerable, I now realize happened that evening when I spoke to my Mom and heard of Dad's passing. I had never felt that open, spacious, helpless, or insignificant. I had also never felt that humble. I had also never felt that profound sense of love and care and self-lessness for not only my dad, but for everyone in my life. I had also never felt what it was like to not be in control. I experienced vulnerability, almost with an emotional depth charge delivered by my father's passing. The reason the choir began to sing better was because I walked into that rehearsal vulnerable, whether I wanted to be or not. From that day on, I have tried to find that place everytime I conduct. It is not easy, but it is necessary. I also believe that dad's funeral caused me to understand who I really was, not who I thought I was, based upon my life, especially before age eighteen. One cannot forget out of hand the formative experiences of one's life and expect to make honest music.

Vulnerability cannot be defined. It can only be described based upon each person's experience. But one has to experience vulnerability in one's own life to know vulnerability. Vulnerability cannot be taught in a classroom. It is taught in life. Each person must search his or her own life for those times when he or she has been vulnerable and then carry those feelings to the podium or to the stage, and, most importantly, to the rehearsal room. I know of many conductors who believe that they are vulnerable in front of their ensembles. They are not, and you can hear it in the sound of their choirs. What you hear is their closure and anger.

I share with you my first experience with vulnerability not as a shining example, but to show that vulnerabilty truly is taught in life. Humbleness, love, care, selflessness, and spaciousness are the all too inadequate words that attempt to describe this remarkable human state. I have learned that in order to access it on a regular basis, I must be able to find stillness within myself. After accessing and understanding stillness (see Chapter 8), it then becomes our charge to carry our life into our music; to be in that vulnerable place taught to us in our lives as we teach, conduct, and perform.

Life: A Straight Line or a Spiral?

Most of us view our lives as a straight line from birth to death. We move at a steady forward pace with life's events providing what we believe to be a consistent momentum. The humdrum of daily life moves the cycle forward. The "busy-ness" of daily routine gives little time for thought or reflection. Consequently, our music making assumes the same characteristics of our life. The music moves forward at a predictable pace. There are few surprises, and it lacks qualities that are born out of contemplation, thought, and stillness. Life moves ahead in a straight line; why shouldn't our music?

One's life should not move forward in a straight line. One's music should not be reflective of this myopic approach. Rather, it is helpful to model one's life after a spiral: an endless circle that moves both forward, upward, and downward, almost like the remarkable double helix which contains the DNA of life. An upward direction continually loves without bias. A downward direction keeps us rooted to our past and our essence and that additionally allows us to deepen our understandings (and acceptance) of ourselves and others. However, before a spiral moves upward and forward, it sets aside time for reflection, rest, and renewal. It is that reflection or quiet/stillness time which moves the life spiral onward. Making time daily to pause to catch our breath and to absorb what we have just done is the most important thing we can do to make music meaningful for us and for those with whom we make music. Music, while reflective of the essences and realities of life, must not get stuck in the things that pull life down. We must make time in our daily lives to absorb what we have done, acknowledge where we are before we move forward. Most of us do not realize that our music becomes static because we become stuck in the relentless forward movement of life in a straight line. We must map our lives in another way. We need to perceive our life and our music as a spiral that allows us time for reflection, stillness, and calm. Out of that reflection, stillness, and calm emerge a new level of music making and human relationships. It is, in essence, taking time in one's life to allow for love and care of self and others to enter into the music-making process that will infuse music making with honesty and human profoundness.

Toward a Definition of Center

Center, as you might imagine, is a very difficult thing to describe. We can learn about a thing by discovering what it is not. This exercise may help you to define center by allowing you to understand what things do not constitute center.

Imagine that you were given the task of writing your own biography. In fact, I will ask you to write four autobiographies. Complete the following exercises.

Exercise One

Write an autobiography entitled *My Musical Journey*. Write the titles of the seven chapters of that autobiography in the form of questions.

Chapter One:

Chapter Two:

Chapter Three:

Chapter Four:

Chapter Five:

Chapter Six:

Chapter Seven:

Exercise Two

Write an autobiography entitled *My Spiritual Journey*. Write the titles of the seven chapters of that autobiography in the form of questions.

Chapter One:

Chapter Two:

Chapter Three:

Chapter Four:

Chapter Five:

Chapter Six:

Chapter Seven:

Exercise Three

Write an autobiography entitled *A Review of My Life This Year: Important Milestones*. Write the titles of the seven chapters of that autobiography in the form of questions.

Chapter One:

Chapter Two:

Chapter Three:

Chapter Four:

Chapter Five:

Chapter Six:

Chapter Seven:

Exercise Four

Write an autobiography entitled *My Professional Journey*. Write the titles of the seven chapters of that autobiography in the form of questions.

Chapter One:

Chapter Two:

Chapter Three:

Chapter Four:

Chapter Five:

Chapter Six:

Chapter Seven:

In looking at the above lists, some commonalities may start to emerge. Many of the same things appear on several of the lists. A few things will appear on only one of the lists. What is important is to understand that your center is defined by you. That is, life revolves around you, you do not revolve and adjust according to life's pressures. If one believes that life is a stage, then a helpful concept is to imagine that each of the lists above is a different life "stage." For each of those stages, the things that you listed revolve around you, and vice versa. Your own awareness of yourself defines you, and consequently the things that comprise center. In your journey to musical vistas, it is important to do this very important work of becoming aware of yourself and what is important to you. Each of these four stages above is important. All function concurrently in your life, with your being at the center of things.

Chapter Four

The Spiritual Presence of the Musician: Spiritual Synergism That Grows Out of Solitude and Being Alive

The essential problem of the sphere of the interhuman is the duality of being and seeing....We may distinguish between two types of human existence. The one proceeds from what one really is, the other from what one wishes to seem. In general, the two are found mixed together. (pp. 65-66)

Whatever the meaning of the word "truth" may be in other realms, in the interhuman realm, it means that men communicate themselves to one another as what they are. It does not depend on one saying to the other everything that occurs to him, but only on his letting no seeming creep in between himself and the other. It does not depend on letting himself go before another, but on his granting to the man to whom he communicates himself a share in his being. This is a question of the authenticity of the interhuman, and where this is not to be found, neither is the human element itself authentic.

Therefore, as we begin to recognize the crisis of man as the crisis of what is between man and man, we must free the concept of uprightness from the thin moralistic tones which cling to it, and let it take its tone from the concept of bodily uprightness. (p. 67)

There are two basic ways of affecting men in their views and their attitude to life. In the first, a man tries to impose himself, his opinion and his attitude, on the other in such a way that the other feels the psychical result of the action to be his own insight, which has only been freed by the influence. In the second basic way of affecting others, a man wishes to find and to further in the soul of the other the disposition toward what he has recognized as the right. Because it is the right, it must also be alive in the microcosm of the other, as one possibility. The other need only be opened out in this potentiality of his; moreover this opening out takes place not essentially by teaching, but by meeting, by existential communication between someone that is actually being and someone that is in a process of becoming. (p. 72)

Martin Buber
The Knowledge of Man

All the arts we practice are apprenticeship. The big art is our life. (p. 83)

M. C. Richards in
Julia Cameron, *The Artist's Way*

The necessary thing is after all but this: solitude, great inner solitude. Going into oneself and for hours meeting no one—this one must be able to obtain. To be solitary, the way one was solitary as a child, when the grownups went around involved with things that seemed important and big because they themselves looked so busy and because one comprehended nothing of their doings.

And when one day one perceives that their occupations
are paltry, their professions petrified and no longer linked
with the living, why not then continue to look like a child
upon it all as something unfamiliar, from out of the depth
of one's own world, out of the expanse of one's own
solitude, which is itself work and status and vocation?
Why want to exchange a child's wise incomprehension
for defensiveness and disdain, since incomprehension is
after all being alone, while defensiveness and disdain are a
sharing in that from which one wants by these means to
keep apart. (pp. 45-46)

> Rainer Maria Rilke
> *Letters to a Young Poet*

Artistic growth is, more than it is anything else, a refining
of the sense of truthfulness. The stupid believe that to be
truthful is easy; only the artist, the great artist, knows how
difficult it is. (p. 9)

> Willam Cather in
> Mark Bryan, *The Artist's Way at Work*

There is an inner and an outer music. When we are
content with the outer shape of things and present them
repeatedly as profound truth we are likely to be dealing
with superficiality but calling it fundamentality. (pp. 166-167)

> Jamake Highwater
> *The Primal Mind*

In contemporary psychological language, efficiency is a
primary mode of denial....Two insanely dangerous consequences result from raising efficiency to the level of an
independent principle. First, it favors short-term thinking—no looking ahead, down the line; and it produces

insensitive feeling—no looking around at the life values
being lived so efficiently. Second, means becomes ends;
that is, doing something becomes the full justification of
doing regardless of what you do. (p. 39)

> James Hillman
> *Kinds of Power*

The new meaning of soul is creativity and mysticism.
These will become the foundation of the new psychological type and with him or her will come the new
civilization. (p.103)

> Otto Rank in
> Mark Bryan, *The Artist's Way at Work*

The center I cannot find is known to my unconscious
mind. (p. 85)

> W.H. Auden in
> Julia Cameron, *The Artist's Way*

Paul Tillich once said that the saint is a saint not because
he is good, but because he is transparent for something
that is more than himself. (p. 91)

> Peter J. Gomes
> *Sermons*

Human salvation lies in the hands of the creatively
maladjusted. (p. 5)

> Martin Luther King, Jr. in
> John Fox, *Finding What You Didn't Lose*

Where there is great love, there are always miracles.
(p.189)

> Willa Cather in
> Mark Bryan, *The Artist's Way at Work*

When a conductor stands in front of an ensemble, he must do infinitely more than just raise his arms. The preparatory position, as it has come to be known, has long been associated with what position one places one's body in order to begin. The arms are in a certain position, the hands assume a shape in a particular way, and the posture of the conductor is usually stressed. While all of the physical positionings are important matters, few if any discuss the more serious issues concerning the spiritual dynamic of the room. That spiritual synergism is set in motion by, and to a great degree fed by, the energy and spiritual presence of the conductor. Music teachers, when they cohabitate the classroom with their students, have the same effect on the students. And, most certainly, the spiritual synergism of performers can be readily felt and experienced by any audience regardless of age or musical experience.

That spiritual presence is manifested to the choir through a body attitude of the conductor that must be rooted in life's experiences. When one stands in front of an ensemble, a line of communication, a life connection is immediately established, or that connection can be immediately destroyed. What is that connection? What does that connection feel like?

There are no specific steps to get to that synergism. However, one can certainly talk about how to access such a place. Accessing is the key. If one can find the way in, each person's unique spirit will transfer to the ensemble, the classroom, or the audience in an electrifying, mystical, and magical fashion. There is nothing more compelling than the human spirit when perceived by others.

How does one access such a spirit? By knowing oneself, believing in oneself, and, above all other things, loving oneself and loving and caring for those with whom one makes music daily. All of this must be born out of solitude, quiet, and inner stillness. One has to spend time each day to be alone with oneself, to allow time to listen to self. This calm and stillness is the most difficult challenge for musicians. If that state of solitary peacefulness can be located, then one simply goes there when music making is about to begin, and stays there throughout the music-making process.

What does it feel like to welcome a meaningful friend, relative, or love when one arrives, for instance, at an airport? Your arms reflexively spring outward. You feel open and receptive and very vulnerable to love and human care. That is the place you must access so that your spiritual self reverberates through your body out toward the choir. Your inside spiritual self is what is perceived by the choir. This spiritual self is not to be confused with ego or personality. Many label this spiritual synergism as the soul of the musician. A great deal of understanding what comprises soul and spiritual synergism is the understanding of what they are not. If one eliminates the ego and personality from the musical synergy of the conductor, teacher, or performer, one has made considerable progress towards a profound relationship with oneself. It is a trust and understanding of oneself which will catapult one into a deeper relationship with oneself. Much of our musical training avoids and, in many cases, ignores growth and development in this area. Hence, while many musicians have developed incredible technical skill, and teachers have developed highly sophisticated teaching methods and strategies, they are devoid of the very spiritual energy which has provided creative impulse in humankind since the beginning of life. One simply cannot grow as a musician without serious and profound work on self in order to access soul. The search to find and understand soul must be the foundation for all musical experience. It is to that end that every musician, regardless of ability or calling, should commit his or her entire being.

Meditation, finding center, and quieting of oneself on a daily basis is the vehicle by which begins and continues the understanding of soul. That is the stuff of this book that one will find in succeeding chapters. When one is able to arrive at the place within oneself where one truly lives, then all one needs to do to "conduct" is to want to share oneself in a very basic, human way with the ensemble. Simply put, one needs to care deeply about each human being that sits in front of them and love them. That is the only condition by which honest music making can occur. The conductor/teacher/performer must be able to stand there and just be.

The Issues for Those Who Receive

As a side issue, it must be said that the ensemble or class also must be prepared to accept and be open to such a sharing. Life experiences do not encourage such openness, care, and loving. The problem is compounded by the complex nature of family life at the end of the twentieth century. If there is not love, care, and openness in the home, then one will have difficulty in the world. While one may be able to function with daily tasks in the world, a musician will be severely handicapped and, in many cases, debilitated as he or she attempts to function as a musician. It is interesting for me to hear choral performances where the conductor is an exquisite teacher. The elements of music have been well taught. Fundamental elements of singing are all in place. There is a rhythmic vitality to the singing. Yet, if one really listens, one can tell that the music is barren of love and care. Music performances can and do take place devoid of such things. But if one can truly listen, one can hear that the music is not about life. It is about everything else. Most of those very same conductors lull themselves into believing that they made music. They manufactured music. Music was not created through the corporate soul of conductor and ensemble. The manufacturing of music goes against life in many cases. It is unfortunate that the conductors involved do not or cannot recognize the differences. In all cases, it has been my observation that such conductors spend little time with themselves and moreover do not trust their own musical voice. They never can let the choir sing. They are constantly controlling the sound (and spirits) of the ensemble. They dictate rhythm and releases in their conducting gestures. Their entire body does not receive the sound as one would welcome a friend or love. As we move into the twenty-first century, conductors, teachers, and music makers must be vigilant to maintain the humanity in what they do. That the music remain a reflection of real life will be a horrendous challenge to all of us. Because of technology and electronic communication, closure of human beings will rise exponentially if we are not careful and committed to this task.

For the ensemble member (and for the conductor) one central issue is understanding what it is to be alive, fully alive, as one makes music. Truly alive human beings are in the world as examples, but one must not only look for them, but recognize them when one comes into contact with them. Allow me to share one example with you. Several years ago, I was traveling the New Jersey turnpike. I stopped at a rest area that had some eateries, one of which was a frozen yogurt establishment. As I approached the counter, there was a long line of nuns waiting to be served. I took my place at the end of the line and waited patiently as did the nuns. As I waited, I noticed a very short nun in front of me. Very unassuming and very quiet, almost prayerful in her patience. Before long, she was at the counter, and I was next. She was served, and turned around to leave. She looked into my eyes, almost into my very soul (she caught me off guard) and said, "God bless you." I was taken aback by her honesty and directness, and, I must say, love. It was clear to me immediately that this "God bless you" carried more than most "God bless yous" I had received before. Instantaneously, without thinking, I immediately responded, "God bless *you*."

After the exchange (and not before) I recognized the spirit. It was Mother Teresa. Yes, Mother Teresa! If there is a definition of holiness, she is it. Her spirit and soul were honestly shared with me, a total stranger. She touched me to what seemed the center of me. I felt open and very vulnerable at that point...because she was. Such is one of the hallmarks of a truly alive person.

Many conductors and many more ensemble members seem all too bored with life. The world has worn them down to the point where they do not react to anything—to people, to sounds, to conversations, to life. Then they come to rehearsal and believe that they can make music in that state. Their insides are noisy to the point that they can't hear their own inner voices. If a conductor knows his own center and can access it and then share it, then those who come into the rehearsal will begin to slowly open. They must be cajoled, prodded, and pushed constantly to commit to the music at hand. Their faces must be alive. The conductor must be alive. There must be care and love in the room. And it can never wane for a moment from anyone. The commitment to soulfulness in the rehearsal born out of solitude must occupy every minute. If that commitment is there, magnificent music that reaches people's souls will be spontaneously created.

A major role of the rehearsal experience should go beyond the teaching of the notes and rhythms. The rehearsal must be a place where the individual singers and instrumentalists understand, too, how to be open toward each other and the conductor. This is very difficult pedagogical turf for any conductor because it is laden with the composite life experiences of all who sit in front of the conductor. Life at the end of this millennium and the beginning of the next does not cultivate openness of spirit and spontaneous human expression. Instead, it breeds closure, protection of self, non-responsibility for any action or deed, mechanistic communication via computers and the Internet, and the harried pace of living. Combine all of those factors, and the result may be difficulty penetrating, much less communicating. Closure is evidenced in persons who hear but do not listen; who do not know spontaneous reaction; who do not understand their emotional make-up because they avoid it. The conductor must work through these issues with the choir by asking them to be fully alive while they sing or play. They need to examine daily what it means to be alive and vital. If they understand what it is to be fully alive, then their music will mirror that aliveness.

Most conductors believe that as they conduct, the following paradigm is in operation:

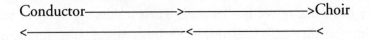

Conductor————————>————————>Choir

As the choir sings, the conductor provides spiritual energy which is then returned by the choir. Such a paradigm places all the responsibility for music making on the conductor, and the choir accepts little if any responsibility for what happens. Their job is merely to "return" what was given to them by the conductor. Allow me to suggest a different paradigm:

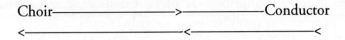

Choir————————>————Conductor

In this paradigm, the choir is held accountable for supplying the energy and soulful synergism in the music-making process. The conductor then actively reacts to their spontaneous human spirits. The choir creates the music, and the conductor actively reacts and evokes from the singers sounds that are born out of their soul. It has been my experience that if the choir is given this responsibility, and is asked to commit to the process in the most profound way, they will accept that responsibility and sing beyond expectations. Such performances then become centered around the lives and souls of the singers and not the ego or personality of the conductor. In such performances, the composer is then given an opportunity to speak.

Toward a Definition of Center

One's center is the internal focus of one's being. It is the place where the experiences of one's entire life reside, but are not compacted or pushed down. Those life events both happy and sad are the place from which truthful music grows and is nurtured. Center is also the place where one's profound life beliefs reside. Beliefs in faith, others, and self all occupy this very sacred place. That place is a wellspring of energy and life that gives music its sinew and core. Center is the place by which you stay both connected to the ground and the earth, and to the world around you. To be alive, you must always be aware of your center. Your center provides stability and strength. It provides the kindling for trust in self and trust of others. Most importantly, one's center is the place from which human love, care, humbleness, selflessness, and giving flow. All that you believe is translated to the choir in an unspoken language.

How does one access center? One accesses center by being in a state of total awareness. You simply work hard to become aware of all of the aspects of center mentioned in the above paragraph. You work hard to know yourself. If you believe that music is self-expression, then you must have some self to express.

This total state of awareness is painful. Many of us are not aware for that very reason and subsequently have no perception of our own center. We avoid the pain of our lives. We detach from others when we need to give more, not less, of ourselves. Instead of deepening in our lives, we become shallow. We push away those who care for us in all aspects of our lives, and make them scapegoats for our own fears. Instead of taking time to go deeper into ourselves and our souls, we reject such a journey and opt for the quick fix which invariably avoids confronting the complexities of life.

As artists, we are complicated and complex human beings. We should appreciate our complexity, respect it, but not use it as an excuse for not knowing or avoiding ourselves and our centers. We need to constantly explore within ourselves life's issues in order to gain clarity concerning our souls, our very spirits. How can one do this? Simply by making time to be with oneself when all is quieted and one can begin to listen to oneself instead of the clatter of the world all around. Whether this soulfulness and spirituality is arrived at through meditation or quiet time is not important. The "how" is not important. The "why" is not even important. It is the exploration of the "who" which forms the core, the center of all music making. Musicians will respond in a powerful, direct voice when the person in front of them knows their own center. Once one knows one's center and has "visited" it often, then that center becomes revealed to the ensemble or to the classroom. What is revealed is the essences of truth, which then becomes translated into musical sound. When this is done, the ensemble is thrust into their own arena of awareness and of center.

Chapter Five
Understanding and Pursuing Center and Soul

We live on the fringe of reality and hardly know how to reach the core. What is our wisdom? What we take account of cannot be accounted for. We explore the ways of being but do not know what, why or wherefore being is. Neither the world nor our thinking or anxiety about the world are accounted for. Sensations, ideas are forced upon us, coming we know not whence. Every sensation is anchored in mystery, every new thought is a signal we do not quite identify. We may succeed in solving many riddles; yet the mind itself remains a sphinx. The secret is at the core of the apparent; the known is but the aspect of the unknown. No fact in the world is detached from universal context. Nothing here is final. The mystery is not only beyond and away from us. We are involved in it. It is our destiny, and "the fate of the world depends on the mystery."

There are two types of ignorance. The one is dull, unfeeling, barren, the result of indolence; the other is keen, penetrating, resplendent; the one leads to conceit and complacency, the other leads to humility. From the one we seek to escape, in the other the mind finds repose. (pp. 44-45)

Abraham Joshua Heschel
Between God and Man

Thomas Merton once remarked that in considering any
important decision in life, it's imperative to "consult your
death" because, as the English writer Samuel Johnson
once put it, "When a man knows he is to be hanged in a
fortnight, it concentrates his mind wonderfully." Death is a
strip search. It points the barrel of mortality at your head
and demands to see what you have hidden under your
garments. It also asks the question, "What do you love?"
As you listen for callings, keep such a question poised in
your mind to help tune out some of the static. In fact,
"What do you love" is the question that callings pose.

Many years ago, I interviewed a number of people who
were forced to consult their deaths because their doc-
tors had told them that they were dying. A few of them
were shattered by the news, but most were liberated.
They spoke about feeling no longer trapped by life, feeling free to speak their minds and follow their hearts, free
from imaginary fears, tyrannical conformities and pleas-
antries, and petty authorities. One woman had told me
that her cancer diagnosis was "not a death sentence, but
a life sentence." She no longer wondered how to spend
her precious nick of time. Her passions and loves were
finally released. (p. 31)

The psychologist Abraham Maslow calls spiritual and
emotional truancy the Jonah Complex: "The evasion of
one's own growth, the setting of low levels of aspiration,
the fear of doing what one is capable of doing, voluntary
self-crippling, pseudo stupidity, mock humility."

"The guilt of Jonah," says Arthur Koestler in *The Act of
Creation*, "was that he clung to the trivial, and tried to cultivate only his own little garden."

If it's any consolation, so does almost everybody when
confronted by a calling, at least initially. Everybody, to

some extent, backs away from their authenticity, settles for less, hobbles their own power, doesn't speak when spoken to in dreams. Everybody occasionally ignores the promptings of the soul and then the discontent that ensues, trying to distract themselves by counting their blessings, all the reasons they ought to be happy with their lot in life, content with things as they are, things that may once have been be-alls and end-alls but that lost their intoxication after five years, put them on automatic pilot after ten, and became a prison after fifteen. (pp.191-192)

We struggle against nothing so hard as coming-to, the author Saul Bellow once wrote, the work of busting the spirit's sleep, and "suffering is about the only reliable such buster-upper, though there is a rumor that love also does the trick." (p. 229)

Gregg Levoy
Callings

In his book, *Kinds of Power,* James Hillman proposes a framework for personal growth. If one has a desire to know oneself better, then it is of primary importance that some strategies be employed by which one can come to understand where within oneself that one lives. This work is not external; that is the type of work that keeps one busy doing "things." That kind of work is easy. The artist with a desire to seek truth in his art must explore truth in himself. The location of that truth within oneself is, many times, hard to access. But be assured that there is basic truth in each of us as human beings. To borrow Hillman's categories, the following five areas can provide routes into one's spiritual core or center.

Deepening
Intensification
Shedding
Repetition
Emptying

Deepening

Plant life grows in the world by putting down roots while at the same time growing above the surface of the ground. As the plant ages, the roots go deeper and reach out horizontally. While we often use the appearance of the plant above the ground as an indication if its health, that fact of the matter is that its true health is determined by the width and depth of its root system. Trees continually push their roots downward while they grow upward.

In human beings, deepening and opening requires of us that we stay the course; in essence, stay with the messes in our lives. When one chooses deepening, one has chosen a path that does not allow for avoidance or escape at any time. Many human beings avoid deepening their entire lives. Artists find that they cannot avoid this important life work. Deepening not only involves new explorations into uncharted territory, but it must also involve constant revisiting of the past life lived. For it is the richness of our lives which brings honesty to the music we make. The pain, happiness, the sorrows—all of it contributes to the deepening process.

Many musicians do not realize that they must make a conscious decision to deepen. They do not realize that they need to constantly work at making their lives deepen in order to arrive at and ponder the most important of life's issues. Those issues are different for each one of us. But it is most often that these basic life issues theater the ones that are expressed by composers in their music. If one has not made deepening journeys into oneself, then it is difficult, if not impossible, to recognize the journeys that are contained within the music. The process of deepening is always difficult and sometimes painful. It requires a stick-to-it-iveness that mirrors commitment but goes far beyond it. Within a musical context, deepening is symbolized by the rehearsal process itself. Repetition in the rehearsal room causes a musician to continue to stay with the music not only to make all things technically right with it but to make the music a part of one's being so that one begins to speak through the music. Most persons, when pressed to stay with the music, give up. They get frustrated, lose attention and focus; many daydream. They refuse (not consciously) to take the journey. One characteristic of deepening is staying power. For most musicians, an inability to deepen musically is symptomatic of an inability to deepen in life itself. Deepening in life precludes deepening in music. However, one can learn about deepening through music. In some cases, if deepening is experienced in a musical situation, it can be used as a paradigm for life.

Intensification

Synonyms for intensification are quality and simplicity. Both of these terms run in the face of living in the modern world. The larger and more complicated something becomes, the more "value" is assigned to the place, event, or activity. Musicians raise the quality of a performance in order to get at the simplicity or the directness of a piece of music. And so they should. Discovering the music through a deliberate, disciplined rehearsal process invariably raises its aesthetic quotient, certainly for the singers, and most importantly for the audience. Intensification that transforms aesthetic levels is directly related to one's ability to love. One can perhaps learn some things by loving the art. But it is much more meaningful to bring the love that one has experienced and is experiencing daily in one's life to the music. If love is not a part of one's life, then one must deepen in order to find out why love is avoided. A musician must love the music, love the work involved in birthing a piece, but most importantly love and respect his or her own intuitive musical voice. James Hillman (1995) summarizes by saying that "what counts in art's intensity is the artist's dedication, passion, enthusiasm, ecstasies, and sweat. There is devotional focus to what you are doing—an intensive concentration that seems like obsession...."(p. 54)

Shedding

Shedding is a more difficult concept to describe. It is difficult to describe because most of us avoid shedding altogether. Sheddings are the most difficult of life's issues to come to terms with. Because most people avoid confronting life's sheddings and moving on, they get stuck in the past. Hence, their music never is able to speak with a voice of clarity because they carry the baggage of non-shedding.

Catastrophic life events call upon us to shed. Divorces, illnesses, and loss of job are just a few examples. These life events hurt, but the shedding hurts even more. Consequently, because of that hurt, we choose not to go there, not to shed. If one is able to shed, one can see the future in a new, positive light. The catastrophic event is not forgotten, but left behind. One moves on and does not constantly revisit the event. You shed the event, ascertain what remains in your life, and move on. You move on with love and care for yourself and all those who are in your life. You avoid melancholy and embrace the day-to-day living of life. In doing so, your music will likewise achieve a freshness, vitality, clarity, and honesty that is unmistakable.

Repetition

For many musicians the act of repetition in the rehearsal process is denigrated. Many tout the necessity of seeing the whole to realize the parts. For those same persons, repetition destroys the whole; one cannot see the whole because of one's incessant perseveration on the parts. The irony in all of this, however, is that great artists are great artists because they enjoy practice as much as performance. That is because their practices (or repetitions) are always performances. Repetition in rehearsal is both repetition and deepening. One must experience focused repitition in order to discover the mysteries of the art. One must experience repetition in order to explore the beauties of the piece. One must repeat in rehearsal in order to learn a fundamental human condition: commitment. Purposeful repetition is fundamental to the development of both the art and the artist. Art cannot develop with the development of the artist. Repetition is the only road in.

The profound dilemma for artists is that the world despises any repetition that adds time to any process. Speed is important. Fast food, e-mail, and computers are contributing to this faster-than-thou attitude. The pace of life is so fast that it is difficult to experience repetition. Repetition seems to slow one's work; it seems, at least at first blush, to avoid completion of the task or arrival at a goal. How do fine craftsmen learn their trade? Through incessant repetition. If one uses repetition to refine, discover, and deepen the musical material, repetition is the way things become beautiful. However, to recognize beauty, one must first know beauty through one's life. Most importantly, one must live for beauty. A singer must want to make a beautiful sound every time he or she sings. If one desires and lives for beauty, then purposeful repetition is the only way that one arrives at beauty. One must, however, fly directly in the face of society as an artist to achieve this. Dig in and dig deeper. Stay the course until the music begins to live. Believe in yourself and believe that you will get there with hard work. The rewards of such activity bring new meaning to life and living.

Emptying

Though there are many synonyms for emptying, the most powerful are stillness and quiet. Literally considered, emptying implies the removal of something, the ridding of stuff. Within a musical and artistic context, emptying should not implying getting rid of "stuff." Rather, it should denote the process out of which music is created. If one has done one's life work—especially with regard to deepening and, as a later chapter points out, mimetics—then one becomes a blank slate similar to the Greek *tabula rasa* concept. It is out of that stillness that music is created time and time again. There has to be sufficient empty (open and vulnerable) interior space so that one can hear one's intuitive musical voice. All artists have this intuitive voice. Many never hear it because they haven't sufficiently "emptied" their interiors so that the voice can speak; in many cases it is overshadowed by the clatter of life issues that have not been confronted and accepted. Most importantly, when one loves, there is a unique kind of spaciousness that grows out of love and care. The way to emptying is to love and care for yourself in order that you may love and care for others in a human way. Another way of thinking about this is to consider the Greek idea of kenotic love. Kenotic love is a love that is self-emptying. Conductors should be in a constant state of kenosis. *They should give and give until they are empty. At the point of emptiness, they will have made themselves so much less that everyone else in the music-making process becomes more.* This, perhaps, is the most important aspect of a musician's musical life. Through the music, one shares and gives love. Music empowered with love has an incredible warmth and beauty of tone that is simply unmistakable not only to the ear but to the heart. The love experienced throughout one's life makes the container for "emptiness" larger and larger. The more love and care are accessed on a daily basis, the more profound and beautiful the music. Such is the stuff that we most often label as "inspiration."

Exercise

This exercise is designed to allow you to begin to articulate feelings or ideas that are intuitive. These intuitive feelings often go unnoticed by many because they have not taken the time to identify them or to spend time with themselves to hear what is inside them. It may be helpful to write down responses to the following questions as soon as you read the questions below. After the entire exercise is completed, then you may go back and read your responses.

Write your responses to the following words:

silence

embrace

trust

shame

anger

passion

solitude

vulnerability

commitment

1. Silence

Silence is _____

_____

_____

Silence is like _____

_____

Occasions in my life when I have experienced silence:

   1. _____

_____

   2. _____

_____

   3. _____

_____

   4. _____

_____

2. Embrace

Embracing is _____

_____

_____

Embracing is like _____

_____

Occasions in my life when I have experienced embracing:

   1. _____

_____

   2. _____

_____

   3. _____

_____

   4. _____

_____

3. Trust

Trust is _____

_____

_____

Trust is like _____
_____

Occasions in my life when I have experienced trust:

1. _____
_____

2. _____
_____

3. _____
_____

4. _____
_____

4. Shame

Shame is _____
_____
_____

Shame is like _____
_____

Occasions in my life when I have experienced shame:

1. _____
_____

2. _____
_____

3. _____
_____

4. _____
_____

5. Anger

Anger is _____
_____
_____

Anger is like _____
_____

Occasions in my life when I have experienced anger:

1. _____
_____

2. _____
_____

3. _____
_____

4. _____
_____

6. Passion

Passion is _____
_____
_____

Passion is like _____
_____

Occasions in my life when I have experienced passion:

1. _____
_____

2. _____
_____

3. _____
_____

4. _____
_____

7. Solitude

Solitude is _____
_____
_____

Solitude is like _____

_____

Occasions in my life when I have experienced solitude:

1._____

_____

2._____

_____

3._____

_____

4._____

_____

8. Vulnerability

Vulnerability is _____

_____

_____

Vulnerability is like _____

_____

Occasions in my life when I have experienced vulnerability:

1._____

_____

2._____

_____

3._____

_____

4._____

_____

9. Commitment

Commitment is _____

_____

_____

Commitment is like_____

_____

Occasions in my life when I have experienced commitment:

1._____

_____

2._____

_____

3._____

_____

4._____

_____

Part Three

THE LARGER PICTURE

Chapter Six
Musicians As Community

Only he who himself turns to the other human being
and opens himself to him receives the world in him. Only
the being whose otherness, accepted by my being, lives
and faces me in the whole compression of existence,
brings the radiance of eternity to me. Only when two say
to one another with all that they are, "It is Thou," is the
indwelling of the Present Being between them. (p. 30)

Martin Buber
Between Man and Man

Our equal and opposite needs for solitude and community constitute a great paradox. When it is torn apart,
both of these life-giving states of being degenerate into
deadly specters of themselves. Solitude split off from
community is no longer a rich and fulfilling experience of
inwardness; it now becomes loneliness, a terrible isolation. Community split off from solitude is no longer a
nurturing network of relationships; it now becomes a
crowd, an alienating buzz of too many people and too
much noise (p. 65).

Parker J. Palmer
The Courage to Teach

Let [the person] who cannot be alone beware of
community. Let [the person] who is not in community
beware of being alone. (p. 78)

> Dietrich Bonhoffer
> *Life Together*

The truth, however, is that man is never alone. It is
together with all my contemporaries that I live, suffer, and
rejoice, even while living in seclusion. Genuine solitude is
not discarding but distilling humanity. Genuine solitude is
a search for genuine solidarity. Man alone is a conceit. He
is for the sake of, by the strength of, unknowingly and
even knowingly involved in the community of man.

Man in his being is derived from, attended by, and direct-
ed to the being of community. For man to be means to
be with other human beings. His existence is coexistence.
He can never attain fulfillment, or sense meaning, unless it
is shared, unless it pertains to other human beings. (p. 45)

> Abraham Joshua Heschel
> *Who Is Man?*

It is the one who fosters genuine mutual contact and
mutual trust, who experiences the other side of the relationship, and who helps his pupils realize, through the
selection of the effective world, what it can mean to be a
man. (p. xix)

> Maurice Friedman
> *Martin Buber, The Life of Dialogue*

All actual life is encounter. (p. 62)

> Martin Buber
> *I and Thou*

I am enormously concerned with just this world, this painful and precious fullness of all that I see, hear and taste. I cannot wish away any part of this reality. I can only wish that I might heighten this reality. (p. 28)

Martin Buber in
Maurice Friedman, editor, *Pointing the Way*

When the pupil's confidence has been won, his resistance against being educated gives way to a singular happening: he accepts the educator as a person. He feels that he may trust this man, that this man is not making a business out of him, but is taking part in his life, accepting him before desiring to influence him. (p. 106)

Martin Buber
Between Man and Man

The perfected man does not interfere in the life of beings, he does not impose himself on them, but he "helps all beings to their freedom"....Through his unity he leads them, too, to unity, he liberates their nature and their destiny, he releases the Tao in them. (p. 55)

To strive for power for power's sake means to strive for nothing. He who seizes empty power ultimately grabs at emptiness... the will to power as power leads from self-aggrandizement of the individuals to the self-destruction of the people. (p. 157)

Martin Buber in
Maurice Friedman, editor, *Pointing the Way*

The extent to which a man, in the strength and reality of the spark, can keep a traditional bond, a law, a direction, is the extent to which he is permitted to lean his responsibility on something (more than this is not vouch-safed to us, responsibility is not taken off our shoulders).

As we become "free" this leaning on something is more denied to us, and out of responsibility must become personal and solitary. (p. 92)

For educating characters you do not need a moral genius, but you do need a man who is wholly alive and able to communicate himself directly to his fellow beings. His aliveness streams out to them and affects them most strongly and purely when he has not thought of affecting them. (p. 105)

Let us realize the true meaning of being free of a bond; it means that a quite personal responsibility takes the place of one shared with many generations. Life lived in freedom is personal responsibility or it is a pathetic farce. (p. 92)

Martin Buber
Between Man and Man

There are two, and in the end, only two, types of faith. To be sure there are many contents of faith, but we know faith itself in two basic forms. Both can be understood from the simple data of our life: the one from the fact that I trust someone, without being able to offer sufficient reasons for my trust in him; the other from the fact that, likewise without being able to give a sufficient reason, I acknowledge a thing to be true. In both cases my not being able to give a sufficient reason is not a matter of defectiveness in my ability to think, but of a real peculiarity in my relationship to the one whom I trust or that which I acknowledge to be true. It is a relationship which by its nature does not rest upon "reasons," just as it does not grow from such; reasons of course can be urged for it, but they are never sufficient to account for my faith. The "Why?" is here always subsequent, even when it already appears in the early stages of the process; it appears, that is to say, with the signs of being added. This does not at all mean that it is a matter of "irrational phenomena." My rationality, my rational power of thought, is merely a part, a particular function of my nature; when however I "believe," in either sense, my entire being is engaged, the totality of my nature enters into the process, indeed this becomes possible only because the relationship of faith is a relationship of my entire being. (pp. 7-8)

The relationship of trust depends on a state of contact, a contact of my entire being with the one in whom I trust, the relationship of acknowledging depends on an act of acceptance, and acceptance by my entire being of that which I acknowledge to be true. (p. 8)

Martin Buber
Two Types of Faith

The traditional Quaker form of silent group worship has no parallel in other religions and has changed very little since the seventeenth century. What others call a religious "service," Friends call "meeting for Worship," emphasizing that there is no liturgy and that worshippers come together as equal participants. But it should be noted that Quaker Meeting is not the only religious tradition of silent worship, that George Fox was not the first spiritual leader to recognize the value of silence. Siddhartha Gautama, known today as Buddha—another young man who left his home to pursue the truth—discovered silent meditation as the route to enlightenment more than two thousand years before George Fox received his message from God. But Quakers are unique in their appreciation of the spiritual power of group silence. If all forms of worship are attempts to transcend the self and find the divine within, Quaker Meeting uses shared silence as a medium of group discovery, as a way of sharing ourselves with others—and with God. (p. 11)

The cultivated ability to hear that voice is the most enduring value of silence. In silence we can discover the divine within, which is universally accessible but speaks to each of us in a unique voice. If we can locate, at the very center of our silence, our individual "still small voice," we will have found our greatest ally in life. Because if we listen to that voice with an open heart, it will guide us through the most challenging crossroads of our lives: in work, in love, in distinguishing right from wrong.

We need only trust the voice that speaks to us out of silence. (p. 15)

Robert Lawrence Smith
A Quaker Book of Wisdom

As good teachers weave the fabric that joins them with students and subjects, the heart is the loom on which the threads are tied, the tension held, the shuttle flies, and the fabric is stretched tight. Small wonder, then, that teaching tugs at the heart, opens the heart, even breaks the heart—and the more one loves teaching, the more heartbreaking it can be. The courage to teach is the courage to keep one's heart open in those very moments when the heart is asked to hold more than it is able so that the teacher and students and subject can be woven into the fabric of community that learning, and living require. (p. 11)

The culture of disconnection that undermines teaching and learning is driven partly by fear. But it is also driven out by Western commitment to thinking in polarities, a thought that elevates disconnection into an intellectual virtue. This way of thinking is so embedded in our culture that we rarely escape it, even when we try. (p. 61)

Parker J. Palmer
The Courage to Teach

Few of us are fortunate enough to be able to understand the rich alchemy that happens when there is a balance between true solitude and true community in one's musical interactions and one's life interactions. Most of us exist as a wild pendulum that swings almost uncontrollably between loneliness and the crowd. This dynamic inertia manifests itself in the music we make, or rather the music we try to make. As musicians, we constantly and dynamically exist in the atmosphere of a larger community. That larger community can be defined as small as one or extend to hundreds. The relationship with an accompanist is community. The relationship with an audience is a community. The relationship between music teacher and classroom is a community. The interaction between a conductor and ensemble is community. But that relationship is much more than a simple interaction or acknowledgment of existence. It must be a union, a bond, a connectedness that brings human beings so close spiritually that they almost become one—equals on the same playing field.

In many ways, it is somewhat easier to begin a relationship with ourselves. If we know anyone at all, we know some things about ourselves. However, therein lies the paradox. We must have more than a passing and fleeting understanding of ourselves. We will be unable to understand great art in the music we perform until we develop and deepen our inner lives. We cannot possibly understand or even know in other beings what we do not know in ourselves.

Many times conductors and other musicians believe that if they "know" the music, that somehow through the performance of that music a connection between themselves and the ensemble and/or the audience will occur. If one profoundly listens, one can hear the disconnection in the sound. The sound is not alive and lacks the vibrancy that comes from many persons connected to both themselves and to the community at large. For conductors, performers, and teachers who desire connection to larger groups, this search for connection can be both daunting and elusive.

But it need not be so. The writings of Martin Buber have articulated both the complexity and simplicity of community and the connection to it. Buber's stunningly simple idea of "I and Thou" can provide the spiritual paradigm for connection to ensemble to happen. At the risk of over simplification, Buber's "I and Thou" asks those of us who make music with communities of people to consider not dealing with a larger group as just that: a large group. Rather, Buber implores us to believe that the conductor, performer, or teacher is connected to each member of the community in a direct, one-on-one, eyeball-to-eyeball, soul-to-soul union. Both are equal. Both are always equal. Both have equal voices. Both have powerful voices. Each listens to the other in a dynamic that is constant. It is almost like there is a spiritual tether or umbilical cord between the conductor and each person in the ensemble. Nothing can stand in the way of the flow of life and music between the two. It is out of those intimate human connections that the community gains a compelling and human voice.

But that connection is not sufficient in and of itself. There must be a binding agent, a paste or glue that prolongs the I and Thou relationship. For musicians, it is and must always be the music. It is the music which provides the tethering material, the truth about life. In his book, *The Courage to Teach,* Parker Palmer speaks eloquently about "the grace of great things." He writes:

> That phrase comes from an essay by Rilke. When I read
> it, I realized that our conventional images of community
> ignore our relationships with great things that call us
> together—the things that call us to know, to teach, and
> to learn. I saw how diminished the community becomes
> when it excludes the grace of great things and relies
> entirely on our own limited graces.
>
> By great things, I mean the subjects around which the cir-

cle of seekers has always gathered—not the disciplines
that study these subjects, not the texts that talk about
them, not the theories that explain them, but the things
themselves. (p. 107)

Music is the binding stuff of community. The community is
nourished by music or "the grace of great things." Without the
"great things," community is reduced to inter- and intrapersonal
relationships that are usually built on outside perceptions rather
than the soulfulness of all involved. Music is the vehicle by which
souls individually examined and explored speak to the world at
large. Human beings communicating directly with one another
through "great things" speak powerfully and with one voice. That
voice will be characterized by the sublime beauty of all the
elements of music, through the unique voice of the composer. As
Buber says, "Community is where community happens."
Community happens when the *I and Thou* connection between
people is always respected and sought. The *I and Thou* connection
nourishes and enriches lives through the vehicles of "great things."
A musician's soul can be explored individually, but it can only
grow and deepen through the nourishment of constant *I and Thou*
connectedness at every moment. Without that lifeline between
souls, there is no art, and more importantly, perhaps, no real life
or living.

Who, then, is the self that performs? What is a choir? What is
an orchestra? What is a string quartet? They are all composed of
all of us, connected in the most direct way via the soulfulness of
each, that gives "great things" a powerful and compelling voice
that speaks through beauty.

Chapter Seven
Influences of a Profound Soul

What we fear in the world is not the evil in it, nor even the evil in ourselves; far more fearful is the good in ourselves, that good being so demanding that we are scared to dare our full capacity. We are afraid of our potential vulnerabilty. We very often forget that if our being is right, our doing will take care of itself. It is always easier to pull in our horns; to play it safe. In other words, not to climb out on a limb. It is always easier to stay where we are, to bury ourselves in our ongoing lives. We know better, but we forget to remember that life needs to expand over and over.

It seems that we need also despair and frustration, sorrows and tragedies. We need them all to keep us in "fighting form." Moral mediocrity keeps people stuck in a safe place while pain throbs all around us. It keeps us from being our fully human selves.

It is necessary to perform as a good musician. We need excellence in performance; but we need excellence in living because music is a product of living. They are not divorced. I have a "coinage" I like to use: psychoschlerosis. It is not hardening of the arteries, but a hardening of the ability to respond...refusing vulnerability. Ask yourself, do your actions and your heart go together?

The great philosopher Martin Buber said "Community is where community happens." It is not the efforts do-gooders do, but it is an eyeball-to-eyeball confrontation… in love. It is easy to be arrogant if we are not careful. Our goal is to keep the communication free and honest. This goes for the performer, for people who sing together, and for audiences who listen together.

One cannot sing cliches or platitudes; but understanding comes out of reality: real life. This is what music is all about.

I like this description of music. I have forgotten where I read it...of [music being] the utmost in God, also meaning that which is beauty, and truth. We are talking of the dynamite of music. "Music is like upright kneeling, silent screaming, motionless dance."

So many times I've looked at my choir and thought that there must be a magic key someplace to unlock this paralysis of spirit. When people reach the end of the line, the end is very sad. No hope, no forward motion, just utter paralysis. All of us have faced this in our groups. The singers try to look like they should, bless their hearts. They try, but they've missed something. You look at their faces; you know how much growth you need yourself. While you know you don't have the answers, but somehow, through the music, through your community together, you find your way. We sing as we are able to sing.

What it comes down to as conductors, or ministers, or teachers, or parents of children....We need to do a very simple thing. *And that is to care more.* It is so simple that it is elusive. Not a saccharine caring, but a deep down caring that is part of commitment. It is the same care that

makes you commit to the human race and to yourself.
                                        Elaine Brown
                                      Alumni Lecture
          May 13, 1988, Westminster Choir College

Who knows, perhaps in the process of change that the
movement for human justice has forced upon us over
the last twenty years, we will grow to the point where
we will be free enough to "speak the truth in love," as
Paul said. Perhaps we will be able to drop our carefully
constructed and maintained facades of cool disinvolve-
ment and give vent to our feelings. We must learn to
grow in dependence, that is, to speak to our needs to
each other in whatever way we best can. In my time
both as a student in the Divinity School and now in the
Memorial Church, I have found the bulk of most interper-
sonal problems to be those of communication. Why can't
we say, "I love you," "I need you," "I fear you," yes, even "I
can't stand you"? These are the hardest words, and
because we know so many words, we use all but the
right ones and nobody understands anybody. If we are to
grow, we must learn to grow together, to lean not only
on Jesus, as the old gospel hymn goes, but to lean on
each other. Here is where our love is put together, here
is where we are liberated to grow in relationship to one
another; here as Paul says, "Speaking the truth in love, we
are to grow up in every way into him who is the head,
unto Christ, from which the whole body joined and knit
together by every joint with which it is supplied, when
each part is working properly, makes bodily growth and
builds itself in love."

When all has been said and done we are speaking about
an interior process, an inner growth that tampers and tin-
kers with the most delicate parts of our machinery: the
heart, the soul, the mind. We are talking about attitudes
and opportunities, a power that is not generated by our

> will but by God's spirit, and this is the last kind of grow-
> ing, the growing in grace, which makes all of the other
> growth possible. It is that unexplainable gift of God him-
> self, the gift of grace, that gives us the capacity to cope,
> to understand, to hope, and to help; so let us grow up
> and grow together toward the light like the plants we
> are. (pp. 40-41)
>
> Peter J. Gomes
Sermons

Great teachers have an uncanny ability to make an imprint deep within a student that goes beyond the teaching of book knowl-edge. In fact, great teachers leave their mark so profoundly that their ideas reappear in your consciousness at the times either when you least expect them or when you need them most. Great teachers not only teach you factual things, but they are able to influence your very center. The irony of study with such persons remains in the fact that, at the time, you have no idea what a pro-found influence they are having upon your being.

I am indeed fortunate to have had two rich and very intense years with Elaine Brown. She was a teacher of humanity and music par excellence, and I will never be able to thank her enough for the deepening way she taught me. This chapter is a meager attempt to let others vicariously participate in the journey on which she took me. What mattered most to Elaine Brown, in ret-rospect, is what should matter most to all of us who live the life of music: to love and care for each other.

Elaine Brown: Biographical Background

Elaine Brown was born in Ridgway, Pennsylvania, March 10, 1910 and passed away on September 6, 1997. She was educated at North Park College, Westminster Choir College, and Temple University. During her long career she served the church, the university, and the community. Throughout her career she was a member of the faculties of Temple University, the Julliard School of Music, Westminster Choir College, and Union Theological Seminary.

Early in her career Elaine Brown had a vision: to bring people of diverse backgrounds together through choral music sung with a high standard of excellence. Her determination to achieve this goal was continually felt in rehearsals, concerts, and workshops across our country and beyond. Whether singing in a facility for prisoners or for the elderly or the homeless, or with the Philadelphia Orchestra on the stage of the Academy of Music in Philadelphia, she was untiring in her efforts to bring music to every segment of the community and to make Philadelphia a "Singing City." She was its Founding Director in 1948 and served in that capacity until her retirement in 1987.

For her commitment to such a vision and professional excellence, Dr. Brown was honored with the Philadelphia Gimbel Award, the Prix d'excellence from the French government, the B'nai B'rith Interfaith Award, and the National Conference of Christians and Jews Award. In the year of her retirement, she received the prestigious Philadelphia Award for "her extraordinary contribution to the Philadelphia community, making a real difference to the city's cultural life."

An Indomitable Spirit

Dr. Brown always remarked that graduate students were one of her greatest challenges. Twenty-two-year-old graduate students are an especially hard lot to teach. In reflecting backwards, I think that I was much harder than the "average." I had come to study with Dr. Brown by a strange turn of fate. I had auditioned for another conductor with whom I had hopes of studying for my masters degree. I appeared for classes in August, and discovered that there had been a resignation and that I would be studying with this woman, Elaine Brown. Little did I know that the change of personnel would change my entire professional life and, in retrospect, shape virtually every idea I have concerning the creation of music with choirs.

I vividly remember the first time I met her. The Temple University Choirs assembled before the opening of classes at a camp to get a head start on learning a new cantata composed by Austrian composer Gottfried von Einem which was commissioned for the thirtieth anniversary of the founding of the United Nations. The orchestra was to be the Vienna Philharmonic, the conductor was slated to be Carlo Maria Giulini, and the baritone soloist was to be Dietrich Fischer-Dieskau.

I arrived at the rehearsal room to find the room impeccably set up for rehearsal complete with a meticulous seating chart. Every seat contained a three-by-five card with the person's name who was assigned to that seat. I initially thought that the namecards were a bit on the overkill side of things, but I would learn later that they played a very important role in a larger philosophical framework of working with people in which Dr. Brown passionately believed.

I found my seat in the tenor section and waited for the start of the rehearsal. I can remember clearly wondering what this woman would be like. Rumors flew around the choir (like they do in most choirs) concerning her age (sixty-five at the time). I wondered whether she would have enough "energy" to conduct this choir of 180 voices. There was a great deal of reluctance within me, but my curiosity was providing staying power. I thought to myself that I could always transfer, perhaps even this semester.

Then it happened. A woman with a head of snow-white hair almost magically appeared in the room. I will always remember her entrance because it both unarmed me and made me a bit uncomfortable. Instead of heading for the podium, fumbling with her briefcase, making small talk with the accompanist, or other such conductor-like things (in my experience), she came into the room looking for us, our eyes, our spirits. She seemingly made instantaneous eye contact with every last person in the room, including me. And it wasn't just a glance. Her being brought a tremendous energy into the room, and her eyes really saw me and everyone else. I felt it. She was briefly introduced to the choir (I later learned that she wanted no testimonial, just her name and a mention, perhaps of Singing City and her prior association with Temple University) and literally jumped onto the podium.

I expected a speech. I wanted a speech. There was no speech. As she stepped onto the podium and opened her score in the same movement, and with an honesty that was shocking to a twenty-two year old, looked directly at the choir, at each one of us with a spirit that was electric and said, "Let's get to work." The forte downbeat was given and we were off.

My first experience with Elaine was not words, but music and spirit. No talk or chatter about her and her reputation or things that would clearly establish control of the room. In the first few minutes I felt as if I had known this woman all my life. I wanted to sing and I worked hard on the music. Throughout the rehearsal, I was strangely aware of only the music and not her. Initially disconcerting, I grew to love the direct contact with the music that for some reason had never been allowed before. There was considerable concern on my part because she also did not rehearse the choir in a way that I was accustomed to, or was expecting! She worked hard at getting the music to speak from us. I also recall trying to analyze why there was so much energy coming from her into the room, almost seemingly through each of us. The room was brilliantly filled with energy. I felt a great deal of responsibility in that rehearsal to the music, which I had not felt before.

After that rehearsal, I had a feeling within me that I can only call "nervously scared." At the time, I didn't know why, but in retrospect, I now know why. Somehow, even though I was one singer out of 180 in that room, Elaine caused me to open myself spiritually in a way that I had never experienced to that point.

I also know that for some reason I opened myself to the sound and to the music, and it scared me profoundly and deeply. And it happened almost magically. All of it was a bit too much to handle for a know-it-all graduate student who wanted to desperately hide behind flashy, meaningless gesture and catchy rehearsal techniques mixed with energy for energy's sake. I wanted falseness and hiding in the rehearsal, a place where I could retreat safely and hide. Elaine would have none of it.

The Sectional Assignment: The First Close Encounter

Immediately after rehearsal, Dr. Brown wanted to meet with all the graduate conducting majors; there were six of us as I recall. We gathered around at her request. I will also not forget my first "close encounter" with her. I introduced myself and she gave me this disarming smile. She asked me where I was from. I replied "near Allentown" (I didn't think she would ever know the small town I was from). Her incredible eyes didn't just look at me, they wanted to look into me! I soon learned that Elaine Brown never just looked at anyone; she tried to see into you. And you could always look into her. I learned much in those two years from those eyes. I know I didn't let her in that day. I knew it and she knew it. I think Elaine formed her lesson plan for me based upon that first human contact with me. I now know that she knew at that moment where our work would begin.

"The choir needs sectionals on this piece. Time to get your hands dirty. Each of you will do a sectional after dinner tonight on the first movement." I broke out into a very cold sweat. I didn't think I could do this. I listened intently to her instructions, which were pretty much a blur. At the end of instructions she made part assignments. "Blue shirt, you take the sopranos, Allentown, you take the altos." I was Allentown, I guess. (I would soon learn about one of Elaine's strange hallmarks. She had trouble with names, but could always remember where you were from. If she didn't remember the town, she would address you by a color of clothing). The meeting was over. I was in a panic, but did not want anyone to know it. I went right up to her and said, "Dr. Brown, I'm very worried about this. I don't really know this score." She looked right into me, grabbed my hand and said, "I know you can do this or you wouldn't be here. Do the best you can for Mr. Von Einem."

In that one sentence and look, I learned that she trusted me. I had never felt that kind of trust before. All of us felt it. For the first time in my musical life, I made no more excuses and I didn't run away. Instead, I didn't eat dinner and found a piano and learned that score. I went from the practice room straight to the rehearsal. I don't remember anything about the rehearsal...except that I felt totally out of control! I never felt out of control (I now know that I controlled everything I conducted; that was conducting to me). As the sectional finished, most of these new faces came up to tell me how well I taught the music. I could not believe it. It seemed like one big improvisation on my part.

Well, in hindsight, that sectional was the first of many things I learned from Dr. Brown. I now know that I was able to do that sectional because she trusted me. Trust is something that prior to that point in my musical life was not part of the music-making equation. Because of the rapidity of the assignment, I had no alternative but to trust myself and go. I didn't have time to question myself or my abilities. I was forced to deal with the music and not with a lot of other meaningless matters. I don't remember a lot of "how-to" things from the rehearsal because I am convinced it was the first time I really listened in a rehearsal. I had to "survive." Because I was constantly thinking about the music and not about myself, I now know that I taught better. I taught better because I was honest. I taught what I knew, and told the choir, when we reached a problem spot, that I didn't know it well enough to help them. I remember asking them to help me. And did they. I couldn't believe how they all worked. The entire experience caused me to stay awake all night pondering what happened in that hour. By the way, after the full rehearsal, I was "escaping" from the room when Dr. Brown called out, "Good work, Allentown...."

The Lessons

As part of my graduate program, a weekly private lesson was provided. The lessons were to last one hour; invariably, they went overtime. I had conjured up an image in my head of what would constitute a private lesson. I drew my conclusions from the many, many applied clarinet lessons I received throughout the course of my undergraduate career. I pictured the lessons as being a weekly session where I would prepare works and then conduct them for Dr. Brown. She would provide feedback and suggestions, and I would apply those suggestions to my study. I also believed that much of the lessons would be devoted to conducting technique and gesture. Almost all my assumptions proved to be wrong.

To be sure, the first lesson dealt with the Bruckner "Ave Maria." But the literature only provided a vehicle, I later learned from Dr. Brown's weekly "explorations," as I would come to call them. I also must add that not unlike students in other graduate programs, we fellow graduate students often compared notes concerning the content and conduct of our lessons with Dr. Brown. None of our lessons resembled each other. For the longest time, I was very frustrated by this and many other things about Dr. Brown's lessons. But in hindsight, it was one of the hallmarks of her teaching. I suspect she had mastered the concept of individualized instruction before it came into vogue in music education.

The lessons quickly left the music at hand. Elaine would pepper you with what I considered at the time to be strange questions. As she asked her questions, she always looked directly into your eyes. My first lessons (approximately two months' worth) dealt with breathing and center. The latter is a major concept of this book, the former the subject of an earlier book. She asked me what the word center meant to me. I do not remember my specific reply, but I do remember Elaine wagging her head from left to right with a bit of a smile on my first answer. She asked the question again, but this time she asked me, "What things bring center to your life?" What a question to ask this twenty-two year old. I flushed and gave her the blank academic stare. She told me that my assignment would be to answer that question in the next lesson. She assigned me two books to read which are legendary among the cadre of Elaine's students: *Zen and the Art of Archery* by Eugene Herrigel and *Centering* by Mary Caroline Richards. With some effort, I found them in a small bookshop in Center City Philadelphia and read them cover to cover that weekend.

I read both books, highlighted them, and made notes. And I spent much time trying apply them to music. I could not make the connection. I felt prepared as I went into the lesson, and thought that my knowledge of the "stories" would get me through the lesson. Well, I was soon to find out that I shouldn't try to "hide" or not be straightforward, direct, and honest with Elaine. Straightforward, direct, and honest, I would soon discover, were some of the keys to discovering where my center was.

The next lesson arrived. I took my scores out of my brief, thinking that she would forget my assignment. When I sat down in her office she asked me immediately, "What do a potter and a musician have in common?" I answered, "Both are artists." "Yes," Elaine said, "but tell me what is similar about their spirits." I am sure that the look on my face told all. Blank. Utterly blank. The association of spirit, spiritual, and musicians had simply never been approached with me...and Elaine knew it.

Elaine's teaching was thought by some to be blunt. It was not exactly blunt, but it was direct, and honest, at times painfully so. Encountering my blank stare, she began to share with me her experiences with center. I remember her saying, "Brother, it is where you live; your center is everything that you have experienced in life." She went on to say that many life experiences are centering: friendships, religion, family, life tragedies, love, and community. Out of those experiences, one becomes more centered. You don't make yourself centered, you are or you are not because of your life experiences. She then told me about physical center. "This one is easy," she laughed. "You root yourself like a tree, and you are always aware where you feel the center of your body; it is similar to the feeling that one gets when someone is trying to push you over. You dig in your heels and seemingly grow roots. That feeling of center is where beat one is. It comes straight down the center of your body...almost like saying gesturally, 'I believe.' You must always work hard to stay in that center, in that sense of rootedness."

A light went on inside my head.

Commitment...rootedness...center...and the alignment of beat one. I thought of the gesture that one uses when one wants to emphasize a sentence that he really means. The gesture is usually very direct, straight in direction, pointed, and usually carries a considerable amount of energy. When one points in this fashion, I thought, one is always "grounded" or "rooted." It made so much sense to think of the conducting gesture in terms of the movements that one uses in life which relay to those that see them commitment and dedication to an ideal or a thought or an opinion.

Now I finally understood why Elaine assigned the Zen book and the Centering book. Both books dealt with the same ideas, but in different situations. In the Centering book, M.C. Richards spent most of the text describing the act of centering as it has to do with a potter physically and spiritually centering himself over the potter's wheel before the clay is thrown onto the wheel. To hit the center while the wheel is moving, the person throwing the clay must be centered. If they are centered, their actions (throwing the clay) will likewise be centered. I realized that when Dr. Brown conducted, I was immediately aware of her center—her spiritual and physical centeredness.

When I tried to conduct Bruckner in that lesson, I could kinesthetically feel that I was not centered. She instructed me, "Conduct from belief...go to the place where you believe and you will find center." The problem that I encountered is that my thoughts stumbled trying to think of many things in life to which I was really committed. I had never connected the word commitment to things I did in life. I just did those things on a day-to-day basis. When I really spent quiet time thinking about those things, they were immediately apparent to me. Commitment to family, faith, and, most of all, commitment to others were very strong within me. While I had strong convictions, it never occurred to me that those beliefs connected to musical ideas.

Over a period of those two years, Elaine returned again and again to the idea of center. Commitment to people was a strong principle of hers. Honest, open communication and expression between herself and every member of the choir were paramount in her thoughts. She asked me in one of those lessons to articulate or define a choir's relationship to the conductor.

I don't remember my response, but I remember her reaction to it: she again shook her head from left to right and provided me with another image. "Too often," she said, "we view choirs as masses or walls of people that we 'conduct.' We tend to conduct anonymously. Imagine, if you will, that there is a piece of string or tether connecting from your center to each person in the choir. In other words, a one-to-one connection with each singer. They are lines of communication from your center to each person in the choir. And it is a two-way street: you communicate to them and they communicate to you on a one-to-one basis. I and Thou, you and me. Honest and direct. There is no other way."

That was the first time I heard the words "I and Thou." In an earlier chapter I discussed the philosophy of Martin Buber. Buber's "I and Thou" was almost Elaine's credo. In fact, I believe it was her credo. She believed so much in the community that a choir is and the connections that are possible within that community and with the conductor. Those lessons where I learned about center were some of the most valuable lessons I ever learned. She applied the concept of center when she heard me conduct the ensemble. She would pepper me with questions concerning the music: "Where is center for Brahms?" "Where is center for Copland?"

I vividly remember so many situations of making music with her, from the Bach *B-minor Mass* to Copland's *In the Beginning*. I can remember a rehearsal of the Copland *In the Beginning* with Dr. Brown. We reached the final page. For any of you that know the work, it is an amazing setting of the Genesis text: "And breathed into his nostrils the breath of life. And man became a living soul, a living soul."

In the initial reading of the work, when the choir sang through the final page, I remember her stopping. She looked seemingly at each one of us and said, "It takes so much belief in life to sing this passage. This page is the essence of our lives and Copland has captured it in a sound." From that point onward, the choir understood profoundly what needed to happen in that passage. And did we sing it!

The Rehearsal

I could write many stories concerning Dr. Brown's work with her graduate students and how she chose to relay certain rehearsal and musical concepts. There is one story, however, that happened to me which changed me and how I approached a rehearsal from that day forward. When this occurred, it was one of the more difficult moments of my musical life, but it has shaped my thought from that point onward.

I was rehearsing for my second graduate recital. I believe that I was rehearsing the Mozart "Sparrow" Mass and the Stravinsky *Four Russian Peasant Songs* for Women's Choir. Dr. Brown sat in on every rehearsal. After each rehearsal, she had scheduled a "debriefing" time where we would talk about the music, the rehearsal, and other pertinent matters.

On this particular day, she sat through my entire rehearsal. I was slightly annoyed because not all the singers came to rehearsal that day (a bad mimetic situation, see Chapter 8). The recital was less than two weeks away. I thought at the time that I was working efficiently and getting at musical matters. After the rehearsal was over, Dr Brown waited until those that had questions cleared the room. Before I could speak, she humanely pointed a finger at me, looked me in the eye, and in a humane tone said, "Liar." Without any further discussion, she left the rehearsal room.

I did not know what hit me. I was devastated. I acted like I didn't know what she was talking about. I went immediately to her office which was adjacent to the rehearsal room. I looked at her. I was visibly shaken by the comment and a bit angry (another bad mimetic situation, see Chapter 8). She looked at me and said, "There was not one note of music made in that rehearsal. That rehearsal was about *you* and not the music. The music is what is important. Those *people* are important. You lied to them musically and, in a way, lied in a human way." She grabbed my hand, looked me in the eye, and reassured me. "You're better than that. At all times be honest with the music and love the choir."

That was one of the major lessons of my time with her. She practiced what she preached. The music was always important. She made herself less so that the choir could be more. But all of us that sang for her felt important: important as musical voices and, most importantly, important as human beings. She threw the gauntlet down on that day and made her line in the sand. Since that day I have worked hard to conduct honest, sincere, and open rehearsals that at all times listen to the musical voices and spirits in the choir. And every day I do a rehearsal, I thank her. One word changed my entire musical philosophy.

In Retrospect

There is not a day that passes where I am not thankful for Elaine's careful and humane teaching of me. She always knew, I suppose, that I was very closed and did not want anyone to see my musical or personal weaknesses. But she had an uncanny ability to cut to the central issues. She taught me that music is made with human beings. A love of community and care for each singer is paramount to any music-making activity. She cared deeply about everyone in her choirs and those who studied with her. Music spoke through her humanity. She was always committed to the music, almost relentlessly, and she demanded the same from all that made music with her. She brought her life experiences to the music and seemingly drew strength for her own life from her music and the choirs. Inspirational is such an inadequate word to describe her, but it is the best available. She was the most remark-able spirit I have ever known. At her memorial service, Dr. William Sloan Coffin told those of us who were gathered that "There will never be another Elaine, but she lives on in her students and those she touched." I am so thankful for my time with her.

> The power of our mentors is not necessarily in the models of good teaching they gave us, models that may turn out to have little to do with who we are as teachers. Their power is in their capacity to awaken a truth within us, a truth we can reclaim years later by recalling the impact on our lives. (p. 21).
>
> Parker J. Palmer
> *The Courage to Teach*

Part Four

CONSCIOUS CHOICES

Chapter Eight
Mimetics and Envy:
The Mimetic Predicament
of the Musician,
The Major Obstacle for
the Creative Artist

If people are not humane, what is the use of rites? If
people are not humane, what is the use of music?

Confucius
Analects 5 : 6

Mimetics is practically synonymous with mimetic desire.
Mimesis evokes desire. Desire constitutes mimesis. (In a
concluding conversation with Girard, he speaks of the
need for another term than "desire" because it is so
intimately associated with the influence of Freud's sexual
theory.) Mimetic desire is a kind of non-conscious imitation of others, but it is important to stress that the word
"imitation" has to be joined with the adjective "appro-
priative" or "acquisitive." Mimesis seeks to obtain the
object that the model desires. The function of culture is
to control and channel this potential conflict over the
object. (p. 290)

Girard does not hold that mimetic desire is inherently bad or destructive. It is the structure and the dynamic enabling human beings to open themselves to the world and engage in loving relationships. (p. 291)

James G. Williams
The Girard Reader

From an interview with Rene Girard conducted by James Williams:

JW: Rene, isn't part of the problem just what you are touching on, that mimesis is really preoperational; and prerepresentational? This is important and is not included in any selections of the Reader. You seem to be saying at times that to break away from the mimetic predicament...

RG: You must change your personality.

JW: But that also requires mimesis, does it not? A mimesis of good, a mimesis of love.

RG: Sure. Part of the problem is with the phrase "mimetic desire." And because of Freud the word "desire" connotes the sexual or the erotic. I said recently that we should be able to substitute some other term...I don't know, perhaps "drive," or elan vital, or even Sarte's "project." Almost any word that could express the dynamism, the dynamics of the entire personality.

JW: Here we seem to be distinguishing different kinds of mimesis. But you don't want to say that, do you? In other words, mimesis is always along a continuum.

RG: That's right. It is something that involves the whole personality. Sartre's idea of the "project" is appropriate in a way, although resorting to Sartre too exclusively would be misleading. Maybe the idea of Kirkegaard, the idea of subjectivity as passionate inwardness and choice, would be helpful...I don't know; whatever the term, something bigger and other than "desire" should be used. "Desire" has, necessarily, that narrow libidinal connotation. (p. 268)

Mimesis, imitation. I . A figure of speech, whereby the
supposed words or actions of another are imitated.

Mimetic, to imitate. .adj.Addicted to or having an aptitude for mimicry or imitation. Also, pertaining to imitation. 2. Characterized by, or of the nature of imitation.
                                                Oxford Dictionary

The notion that we can transfer our guilt and sufferings
to some other being who will bear them for us is familiar
to the savage mind. It arises from a very obvious confusion between the physical and the mental, between the
material and the immaterial. Because it is possible to shift
a load of wood, stones, or what not, from our own back
to the back of another, the savage fancies that it is equally
possible to shift the burden of his pains and sorrows to
another who will suffer them in his stead. Upon this idea
he acts, and the result is an endless number of very
unamiable devices for palming off upon someone else
the trouble which a man shrinks from bearing himself. In
short, the principle of vicarious suffering is commonly
understood and practiced by races who stand on a low
level of social and intellectual culture. (p. 624)
                                                J. G. Frazer
                                                The Golden Bough

In music everything is prolonged, everything is edified and
when the enchantment has ceased, we are still bathed in
its clarity. Solitude is accompanied by a new hope and pity
for ourselves, which makes us more indulgent and more
understanding, and the certitude of finding something
again, that which lives forever in music. (p. 63)
                                                Nadia Boulanger in
                                    Don G. Campbell, *Master Teacher*

The soul is born in beauty and feeds on beauty, requires beauty for its life. (p. 39)

Beauty is not an attribute like a fine skin wrapped round a virtue, merely the aesthetic aspect of appearance. It is the appearance itself. Were there no beauty, along with the good and the true and the one, we could never sense them, know them. Beauty is an epistemological necessity; it is the way in which the Gods touch our senses, reach the heart, and attract us into life. (p. 45)

We can respond from the heart, reawaken the heart. In the ancient world the organ of perception was the heart. The heart was immediately connected to things via the senses. The word for perception or sensation in Greek was aisthesis, which means at root a breathing in or taking in of the world, the gasp, "aha," the "uh" of the breath in wonder, shock, amazement, an aesthetic response to the image (eidolon) presented. In ancient Greek physiology and in biblical psychology the heart was the organ of sensation: it was also the place of imagination. The common sense (sensus communis) was lodged in and around the heart, and its role was to apprehend images. For Marsilion Ficino, too, the spirit in the heart received and transmitted the impression of the senses. The heart's function was aesthetic. (p.107)

To move with the heart toward the world shifts psychotherapy from conceiving itself as a science to imagining itself more like an aesthetic activity. (p. 112)

James Hillman
The Thought of the Heart and the Soul

Who are you? Jesse Jackson has identified the greatest cause of social decay in America today, and it is not racism, it is not poverty, it is not drugs, it is not war, nor is it violence. Those are all symptoms and consequences, but they are not the root cause of the greatest social decay in our America today. The cause is a lack of self-worth, a lack of an identity worth respecting, a lack of self-respect and self-dignity, and that comes from not knowing who we really are. (p. 123)

Peter J. Gomes
Sermons

We have to trust these feelings. We have to trust the invisible gauges we carry within us. We have to realize that a creative being lives within ourselves, whether we like it or not, and that we must get out of its way, for it will give us no peace until we do. Certain kinds of egotism and ambition as well as certain kinds of ignorance and timidity have to be overcome or they will stand in the way of the creator. And though we are well thought of by others, we will feel cross and frustrated and envious and petulant, as if we had been cheated, somehow, by life. (p. 27)

M. C. Richards
Centering in Pottery, Poetry, and the Person

For religious man, space is not homogeneous; he experiences interruptions, breaks in it; some parts of space are qualitatively different from others. "Draw not nigh hither," says the Lord to Moses, "put off thy shoes from thy feet, for the place whereon thou staidest is holy ground." (Exodus 3:5). There is, then, a sacred space, and hence a strong, significant space; there are other spaces that are not sacred and so are without structure or consistency, amorphous. Nor is this all. For religious man, this spatial non-homogeneity finds expression in the experience of an opposition between space that is sacred—the only real and real-ly existing space—and all other space, the formless expanse surrounding it. (p. 20)

> Mircea Eliade
> *The Nature of Religion: The Sacred and the Profane*

Real understanding does not come from what we learn in books; it comes from what we learn from love of nature, of music, of man. For only what is learned in that way is truly understood. (p. 210)

> Pablo Casals in
> David Blum, *Casals and the Art of Interpretation*

And when the woman saw that the tree was good for food, and that it was pleasant to the eyes, and a tree to be desired to make one wise, she took of the fruit....

> Genesis 3:6

A good model will make our mimesis good (Christ); a bad model will make our mimesis rivalrous. (p. 269)

> James G. Williams
> *The Girard Reader*

Goethe's ideas about plants, whether botanically accepted or not, nonetheless invite our attention to what is not there. Even further: what is not there characterizes the particular nature of each kind of plant. This idea claims that emptiness has an invisible power that plays a determining role in what appears. Patterns emerge and grow out of the empty, much as the potter's jar forms itself around the active presence of a hollow. Each container—pot, vase, jug, cup—is simply the external shell of a specifically shaped void. The power is in the void. That nature abhors a vacuum may be only a modern Western idea of nature. Different schools of Buddhist thought, for instance, consider the seeds of all existing things to be

contained in a substratum void, so that care for emptiness is what allows the seed to emerge. (p. 61)

James Hillman
Kinds of Power

Meditation is like the pacification of turbulent waters by
pouring oil over them: no waves are roaring, no foams are
boiling, no splashes are spattering, but a smooth, glossy
mirror of immense dimension, and it is this perfect mirror
of consciousness that myriads of reflections, as it were,
come and go without ever disturbing its serenity. (p. 266)

Soyen Shaku
The Practice of Dhyana

But if in the beginning of his life of stillness a man does
not experience the power of such divine visions because
of his mind's distraction, and he cannot yet raise himself
up toward the power of the aforesaid wonders of God,
let him not become despondent and abandon the serenity of his quiet life. For when the husbandman is sowing
the earth he does not immediately see the ear as he
sows the seed; for despondency, hardship, painful limbs,
cutting off friendships, and separation from acquaintances
accompany the work of sowing. But after a man has
endured these things, another season comes wherein the
husbandman is filled with gladness, leaps, exults, and
rejoices. And when is this? When he eats the bread fur-
nished by his own sweat and his rumination is held fast in
stillness. For stillness and the aforesaid patient meditation
enjoyed therein kindle great and endless sweetness in the
heart and swiftly draw the intellect to unspeakable aston-
ishment. Blessed is the man who perseveres in stillness,
for before him is opened access to this divinely flowing
spring; he has drunk from it and been sweetened, and
without cease he will drink therefrom, always and at
every hour of the night and day, until the completion and

the end of this, his temporal life.

Question: What embraces all the labours of this work, that is to say, stillness, so that when man has attained it, he can know that he has reached perfection in his manner of life?

Answer: When a man is deemed worthy of constant prayer. For when he reaches this, he has reached the pinnacle of all virtues and has become a dwelling-place of the Holy Spirit. For unless a man has received in all certainty the grace of the Comforter, he will be unable to perform constant and unceasing prayer restfully. When the spirit dwells in a man, as the Apostle says, he never ceases to pray, since the spirit himself always prays. Then, whether he sleeps or wakes, prayer is never separated from his soul. If he eats, or drinks, or lies down, or does something, or even in deep slumber, the sweet fragrances and perfumes of prayer effortlessly exhale in his heart. He does not possess prayer in a limited way, but even though it should outwardly still, at every moment it ministers within him secretly. For the silence of the limpidly pure is called prayer by one of the Christ bearers, because their thoughts are divine motions. The movements of a pure heart and mind are gentle cries, whereby the pure chant in a hidden manner to the Hidden God. (from Homily 37)

Saint Issac the Syrian
The Ascetical Homilies of Saint Issac the Syrian

Fr. Zosima:
Fathers and teachers, I ask myself: "What is hell?" And I answer thus: "The suffering of being no longer able to love." Once in infinite existence...a certain spiritual being, through his appearance on earth, was granted the ability to say to himself; "I am and I love." Once, once only, he was given a moment of active, living love, and for that he

was given earthly life with its times and seasons. And what then? This fortunate being rejected the invaluable gift, did not value it, did not love it, looked upon it with scorn, and was left unmoved by it. This being, having departed the earth, sees Abraham's bosom, and talks with Abraham...and he beholds paradise, and could rise up to the Lord, but his torment is precisely to rise up to the Lord without having loved, to touch those who loved him who disdained their love. For he sees clearly and says to himself: "Now I have knowledge, and though I thirst to love, there will be no great deed in my love, no sacrifice, for my earthly life is over, and Abraham will not come with a drop of living water...to cool the flame of the thirst for spiritual love that is burning in me now, since I scorned it on earth; life is over and time will be no more! Though I would gladly give my life for others, it is not possible now, for the life I could have sacrificed for love is gone, and there is now an abyss between that life and this existence." People speak of the material flames of hell. I do not explore this mystery, and I fear it, but I think that if there were material flames, truly people would be glad to have them, for, as I fancy, in material torment they might forget, at least for a moment, their far more spiritual torment.

Fyodor Dostoevsky
The Brothers Karamozov

The awareness of grandeur and the sublime is all but gone from the modern mind. Our systems of education stress the importance of enabling the student to exploit the power aspect of reality. To some degree, they try to develop his ability to appreciate beauty. But there is no education for the sublime. We teach the children how to measure, how to weigh. We fail to teach them how to revere, how to sense wonder and awe. The sense for the sublime, the sign of the inward greatness of the human soul and something which is potentially given to all men, is now a rare gift. Yet without it, the world becomes flat and the soul a vacuum. (p. 34)

The Greeks learned in order to comprehend. The Hebrews learned in order to revere. The modern man learns in order to use. (p. 34)

> Abraham Joshua Heschel
> *God in Search of Man*

Nor is it merely that we can discern in Christ that close union of personality with perfection which forms the real distinction between the classical and romantic movement in life, but the very basis of his nature was the same as that of the nature of the artist—an intense and flamelike imagination. He realized in the entire sphere of human relations that imaginative sympathy which is the sphere of Art is the sole secret of creation. He understood the leprosy of the leper, the darkness of the blind, the fierce misery of those who live for pleasure, the strange poverty of the rich. (p. 85)

> Oscar Wilde, "De Profundis," in
> Thomas Moore, *The Education of the Heart*

Many people want to get rid of their painful feelings, but they do not want to get rid of their beliefs, the view-points that are at the very root of their feelings. (p. 56)

Anger is rooted in our lack of understanding of ourselves and of the causes, deep seated as well as imme-diate, that brought about this unpleasant state of affairs. Anger is also rooted in desire, pride, agitation and suspi-cion. The primary roots of our anger are in ourselves. Our environment and other people are only secondary. (p. 61)

If someone needs to be helped or disciplined, we will do so out of compassion, not anger and retribution. If we

genuinely try to understand the suffering of another person, we are more likely to act in a way that will help him
overcome his suffering and confusion, and that will help
all of us. (p. 81)

Thich Nhat Hanh
Peace Is Every Step

What is important is not to define, but to act. One
must try to do one's work with enough love and enough
care to make it represent one's very best. The whole joy
of being a human being is to realize the difficulty in
reaching one's aim. The higher the aim, the greater the
difficulty, and the greater our humility and joy. As for
beauty—it is not mainly through beauty for service, of
which there is no material reward or punishment, that
we reach the spiritual art of our life which is the whole
purpose of existence and its only goal. (p. 67)

Nadia Boulanger in
Don G. Campbell, *Master Teacher*

One cannot force oneself to love; but love presupposes
understanding, and in order to understand, one must
exert one's self. (p. 65)

Igor Stravinsky, "Poetics of Music," in
Thomas Moore, *The Education of the Heart*

I also maintain that those who are punished in Gehenna
are scourged by the scourge of love. Nay, what is so bitter
and vehement as the torment of love? I mean that those
who have become conscious that they have sinned
against love suffer greater torment from this than any fear
of punishment. For the sorrow caused in the heart by sin
against love is more poignant than any torment. It would
be improper for a man to think that sinners in Gehenna
are deprived of the love of God. Love is the offspring of

knowledge of the truth which, as commonly confessed, is
given to all. The power of love works in two ways: it tor-
ments sinners, even as happens here when a friend suffers
from a friend; but it becomes a source of joy for those
who have observed its duties. Thus I say that this is the
torment of Gehenna: bitter regret. But love inebriates the
souls of the sons of Heaven by its delectability. (Homily 28)

Saint Issac the Syrian
The Ascetical Homilies of Saint Issac the Syrian

You must know how to make in yourself a complete
silence. Each of you in my mind is fated. You were born,
you will live, you will die. Even to try is an achievement.
Giving yourself completely is such a faith. (p. 84)

Nadia Boulanger in
Don G. Campbell, *Master Teacher*

We have come here to learn about spirituality. I trust
the genuine quality of this search but we must question
its nature. The problem is that the ego can convert
anything to its own use, even spirituality. Ego is constantly
attempting to acquire and apply the teachings of spirituality for its own benefit. The teachings are treated as an
external thing, external to "me," a philosophy which we
try to imitate. We do not actually want to identify with
or become the teachings. So if our teacher speaks of
renunciation of ego, we attempt to mimic renunciation of
ego. We go through the motions, make the appropriate
gestures, but we really do not want to sacrifice any part
of our way of life. We become skillful actors, and while
playing deaf and dumb to the real meaning of the teachings, we find some comfort in pretending to follow the
path.

Whenever we begin to feel discrepancy or conflict
between our actions and the teachings, we immediately

interpret the situation in such a way that the conflict is smoothed over. The interpreter is ego in the role of spiritual advisor. (p. 12)

Chögyam Trungpa
Cutting Through Spiritual Materialism

Unfortunately, envy enters into the life of every person. Artists are especially susceptible to the negative influences of envy. Envy, if not kept in perspective, can control and influence both the spirit and the music. In fact, envy has become so common to us that it often goes unchecked within us. It becomes second nature. Envy becomes a regular part of everything that we do. We are constantly envious. What do musicians envy? Envy in musicians can be categorized as follows:

> **Envy of the Perfect Sound**
> **Envy of Others' Musical Skills**
> **Envy of Others' Artistry**
> **Envy of Others' Creative Spirits**
> **Envy of Others' Technical Skills**

At the start of this chapter, two words were defined using definitions from the Oxford Dictionary. The word *mimetic* comes from the Greek meaning to imitate. One is mimetic when one imitates the words or actions of others. *Mimesis* also means to imitate, but the definition also includes the statement "addicted to or having an aptitude for mimicry or imitation."

Mimetic Theory was developed by Réné Girard for use in both literary criticism and Biblical criticism. His theories are very relevant to musicians. In fact, I believe that mimetic desire in some form is at the root of the musical problems of most musicians, especially conductors.

Envy is pervasive throughout all aspects of our lives. The envy of things, persons, and abilities causes huge firestorms in our lives. While one may think that envy is a psychological problem, in actuality it poses a spiritual dilemma of the greatest magnitude, yet goes unnoticed in us. As we conduct we pose questions of ourselves. What do they (the choir) think of me? I would like to have her abilities. I wish I could hear as well as he does. The questions go on and on. All are questions of desire and of envy. To satisfy that mimetic desire, we imitate in order to either reflect or acquire those qualities.

Conductors can be especially vulnerable to mimesis in the context of dealing with an ensemble. An improper mimesis can, at the very least, hinder the music making of the ensemble, or at its most severe, cripple and handicap an ensemble. A bad mimesis can also be present in a conducting classroom, a private voice lesson, or in the general music classroom. No musician can avoid, without conscious effort and education, the debilitating effects of a bad mimesis.

The Mimetic Triangle

A mimesis is always generated within a conductor within a three-sided relationship. The conductor is on one side of the triangle. On the highest point of the triangle are the things of which the conductor is envious. Most conductors are envious of the sound that is "in their head." When the ensemble creates a sound, the conductor's mind unconsciously compares that new sound that was sung to a model sound that he/she hears. As a human being and an artist, the conductor desires and wants beauty. Consider the following paradigm:

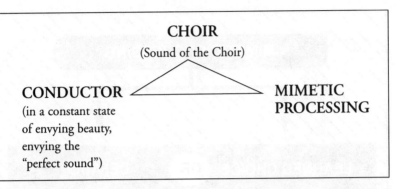

At that moment, the conductor has an instantaneous choice to make. A bad mimesis occurs when no choice is made. When the conductor hears the sound, he has the power to make the conscious decision which will have a major impact on the sound in the room. The options for mimetic processing (choice) within the conductor are shown on the following page.

Mirrored Mimesis

At the moment the sound is created from the ensemble, the conductor, almost unknowingly, is envious of the "perfect sound." When the perfect sound is not created by the ensemble in the hearing or audiation of the conductor, the mimetic cycle is instantaneously set in motion. It is at this exact moment that the conductor must consciously choose the correct mimetic path. He must go to the place that is loving, caring, selfless, self-emptying, helping, and trusting. If he does not consciously and willfully choose the above, human nature will thrust his spirit to a place of anger, mistrust of the ensemble, mistrust of self, inhumaness, varying degrees of violence both in gesture and words (especially gesture), and a general state of frustration. The most predominant characteristic of a bad memesis in a conductor or musician in general is self-mutilation. This usually characterized by "feeling bad" about a rehearsal. One feels badly because the rehearsal went poorly because the singers were not prepared for the rehearsal or were not "being responsible." The resulting sound from the ensemble

MIMETIC PROCESSING

LEARNED CHOICE **OR** **DEFAULT**

love
care
selflessness
allowing
acceptance of self
acceptance of others

want to be perfect
anger
self-mutilation
mistrust of ensemble
mistrust of self

self-emptying love
helping
trust of ensemble
trust of self
ensouling of self
ensouling of ensemble

inhumaness
acts of inhumanity
violence
violent frustraton

SCAPEGOATING

DEVELOPING A COVER STORY

in a situation of a bad mimesis is a phenomenon I like to call a *mirrored mimesis*. That is, what the conductor hears in the sound, in essence, is the reflection of his own mimesis. It is a reflection within the choir of the wrong mimetic choice, either consciously or unconsciously made by the conductor. The ensemble will always reflect the mimetic energy of the conductor regardless of their individual mimetic situations in life. In other words, the mimesis of the conductor tends to override the individual mimeses that each singer may bring into the rehearsal or the performance and is multiplied in its intensity in direct proportion to the numbers of people in the choir.

So how might the conductor handle or attempt to deal with such a mimetic situation? Without conscious choice and the choosing of those qualities which will provide for a good mimesis, a scapegoat is selected by the conductor. In scapegoating, the conductor may focus his attention on one singer or a group of singers. One person or a small group within the larger group is "destroyed" in order to achieve cohesion. The larger the group, the larger the sacrifice will be. As René Girard states, this situation is "unity minus one." Most conductors justify such destruction by rationalizing that it is "for the good of the music and the composer." In essence, a double scapegoat occurs. Not only is the conductor "taking out" his frustrations on the ensemble, but he further complicates matters by using the music as an additional scapegoat for his actions. The next step is that the sacrifice is then rationalized in order to avoid guilt. "They are bad, they deserve it" is one such approach. This can be called a "cover story." Such cover stories allows us to keep hidden from ourselves the true reality, truth, and honesty in the choir. Left untended, this "scapegoat dynamic" can destroy an ensemble and eventually the conductor, and can cripple music making. Ultimately, the music suffers the most.

By engaging in such scapegoating, the conductor in essence conceals himself from the choir. His mimetic desire overcomes the music. Angular, almost violent gestures are the first manifestations of poor mimetic choice. Second, the conductor may engage in a type of self-laceration where he is the scapegoat instead of the choir. At all costs, the conductor must avoid magnifying the crowd mentality that can be set in motion by envy of "the perfect sound."

Why do we envy the perfect sound? Because as artists, we inherently love beauty in sound and in art. Beauty is a major reason for our existence. It is not difficult to understand, therefore, that the striving for beauty in our lives and in the rehearsal room and concert hall can inadvertently fuel the mimetic furnace of the choir.

How to Make the Right Mimetic Choice: The Path to a Good Mimesis

It appears on the surface that choosing a good mimetic path rather than a wrong one is an easy matter. It is not. Choosing the proper mimetic path is not only a musical issue, but it is a profound life issue which will change the quality and interiority of one's life. The world around us does not reinforce correct mimetic choice. It more often than not reinforces the wrong mimetic path or choice. Moreover, our educational process does not reinforce, teach, or support correct mimetic choices. When such mimetic choices are taught, they are usually taught as occurrences outside the person; occurrences that are out of the control of the person, rather than being internal, soulful, and conscious choices.

So how do you acquire a good mimesis? You *will* it. You consciously choose it and push yourself to go there and stay there. Stay there during every minute of the rehearsal. Stay there every minute of the warm up before the concert. Be there throughout the entire concert. Acquiring the correct mimesis is a matter of choice and in that way it is similar to the choices in life itself. Another way to think about this is that throughout the rehearsal and performance process, you must become less. The choir must become more and you must dwindle to the point that you reduce yourself to a real person. As a conductor, you publicly exhibit the unmaking of a bad mimetic personality in front of people so that they became more.

> All creative thinking comes out of an encounter with the unknown. We do not embark upon an investigation of what is definitely known, unless we suddenly discover that what we have long regarded as known is actually an enigma. Thus the mind must move beyond its shell of knowledge in order to sense that which drives us toward knowledge. It is when we begin to comprehend or to assimilate and to adjust reality to our thought that the mind returns to itself. (pp. 114-15)
>
> Abraham Joshua Heschel
> *God in Search of Man*

We have many choices to make in life, and, for the most part, we make them. When confronted with the sound from a choir, remember always that on a deep, profound, and subconscious level you will "envy" the beautiful. The envy of the beautiful sounds in life through music are what makes us musicians. The human need for beauty in music for most of us drives our motivation to become better musicians and performers. In the struggle toward acquiring or experiencing perfection, we focus on all the technical aspects of our art. Conducting technique, singing technique, and analysis seem to be at the core of all curricula. Often, too, we talk about the interpretation of the music. Unfortunately, seldom do we talk or ponder the implication of that music on our lives. How does the piece of music that we are performing impact our life experience and those that hear our choirs? Does the performance speak to profound life issues that know no religious or ethnic boundaries?

To find answers or begin to understand any piece of music, one must bring one's own humanity to bear on the music. A prerequisite to any interpretation is a person's ability to love others, care for others, and have the ability to be, at all times, humble and selfless during both the rehearsal process and the performance. I know conductors who are gifted teachers and talented musicians. But every time I hear their choirs, there is a hardness to the tone that is a result of their inability to love and care for people during the rehearsal process. These persons are also generally cynics because they constantly engage in bad mimetic processes by criticizing every other musical performance they hear. They are critical of colleagues and have a general inability to respect what others can offer. They are also unable to see themselves embroiled in this terrible mimetic predicament. They use the sheer force of their technical musicianship and control to bring about musical performances. Love, care, humbleness, and selflessness must be a constant during rehearsal. They should not be "turned on" for the performance.

Simply put, to place yourself in a good mimesis or good mimetic situation, you need simply to tell yourself that you will love and care during the music rehearsal and performance process. First and foremost, you will love yourself and your gifts, recognizing and accepting your musical weaknesses with love. You also, at all times will be humble and selfless, and place your own ego in a place that does not infect or interact with the music-making process. You will yourself to care more and love more. You will constantly self-empty, love, and care for others. This self-emptying process is known as kenosis. When one is in a state of constant self-emptying love, one is said to be kenotic. It is kenosis for which conductors must strive, without engaging in self-mutilation when they falter. Constant struggle to keep oneself in a good mimetic place is a lifetime journey. To make that journey is, indeed, difficult. To not ever begin to take the journey is a mistake. Ultimately, a bad mimesis will profoundly inhibit and damage, and in some cases, not only hurt the music, but profoundly hurt people.

Solitude and Quiet: Gaining Access to a Good Mimesis

Most persons reading this book, including the person who wrote it, will discover, upon gaining knowledge of this theory, that bad mimesis is, unfortunately, a vital part of everyday life. In fact, musicians will find, to their dismay, that it is a dominant factor in all rehearsal and performance situations. Being aware of bad mimesis is half the battle. Once one realizes that bad mimetic choice is a part of one's musical thumbprint, one can move toward change. The author's experience is that the change is dramatic and life changing. However, gaining access to the correct mimesis is difficult.

Access can only be gained through quiet and stillness within oneself. Quiet solitude must be a daily occurrence. Stillness is a deliberate choice. One must consciously choose stillness. Unfortunately, the world will not give it to you. Additionally, you will have to choose stillness over and over again in very difficult situations where it might be easier not to choose stillness. Initially, the discovery of stillness within oneself brings great joy. Soon, however, it brings difficulties and darkness. One will discover that by being still, the newfound stillness unmakes personality so that one can become a person. By being still, you are able to make yourself less so that others can become more. Also by being still, the process of making yourself less allows the music to speak clearly through the ensemble.

> Now, let us say a good word about depression. Sometimes it is good to be depressed, and we enjoy it, and I don't care what shrinks and therapists say, there are times when it is good to feel bad. For that moment, the only pleasure that we have is in the recalling of our woes, and the capacity to name our fears and to feel them indicates to us that at least we are not as far gone as we might appear to others. There is nothing worse than a friend or colleague who wants to help us out of our pit before we are ready to be helped, and in some perverse sense the frus-

tration of their efforts adds little to our pleasure. It is said
that Abraham Lincoln was at his best when in the midst of
his frequent depressions, and the genius of Martin Luther
is that he was both depressed and constipated. The black
moods of genius have given much beauty, power, and purpose to the world. It is possible to think of depression, at
least in its primary stage, as one of the few places of
autonomy and self-preservation for one on whom the
world appears to be closing in, and like pain it can from
time to time be redemptive. (p. 160)

Peter J. Gomes
Sermons

There must be a time before rehearsal and performance where
the conductor (and the choir) are quiet in order to set proper
mimetic acquisition in motion. The audio tape meditations that
are available with this text are guided journeys to that place which
must be accessed daily until it eventually becomes second nature.
The author suggests that one uses the tapes daily to quiet oneself
and to explore one's center.

How would one describe that inner place? That place is
spacious in feeling and calm. It is a place where the day-to-day
issues of life are kept in perspective. It is the place where one's
inner voice speaks and can be heard. That inner place is the place
where trust in self resides. It is also the place where profound
human love and care are always in residence. It becomes the place
from which one creates all music.

That inner place is a place of utter stillness. To choose stillness
is a deliberate choice. You must make the conscious choice to be
still. Moreover, the world will not give it to you. During life, you
are continually challenged to choose it again and again in very difficult situations. Initially, accessing this stillness will bring great
joy and freedom, but in time, it becomes more difficult. You will
experience a very ordinary peacefulness. This peacefulness provides a sobriety of context, and, in all likelihood, the first sobriety

since childhood. The constant acquiring of stillness unmakes personality so that you can become a person. Who you are as a person can be subordinated to nothing.

What Is a Person?

It seems to me that before one can begin to understand oneself, one must attempt to understand what it means to be a person. Defining a person is not an easy task, and has been discussed and studied by many people. Our personhood is the most precious thing that we possess. So how may a person be defined? Can any of us define in somewhat objective terms what characteristics make up this complete whole we call a person?

Freedom

The first condition of personhood is freedom. Freedom from not being considered a person by anyone. You are a person from birth and you are absolutely unique and irreplaceable. You do not, all of a sudden, become a person. You are one. Many of us lose sight of our own personhood. We see ourselves not as persons, but as things in a larger gameboard of life, somehow being moved around like chess pieces. Who you are as a person cannot and should not be subordinated to any other person, pressure, or thing. However, the irony of personhood is that you can (and do) choose to not act like a person. On the other hand, you can also choose to call yourself to personhood. Understanding what it is to be a person and to respect the personhood of another is one of the greatest challenges to musicians, regardless of medium. If one simply makes the effort to recognize each of the persons in his choir as a person, much progress will be made in the music-making process. Recognizing personhood is one of the most important functions of an ensemble conductor.

Lack of Isolation of the Person

Second, a person does not exist in isolation. Personhood requires that one give to others freely without feelings of compulsion to share. You give of yourself because you want to and need to as a human being. Within that decision to come out of yourself in love is where your personhood is. To give of yourself in any situation is known as full kenotic love. Kenotic love, by definition, is a completely self-emptying love. Establishing this condition of kenotic love, through conscious decision, establishes the optimum mimetic condition. The irony of personhood is that as persons, we want to be admired, not loved. The true person, or the soul of a person, cannot be manifested to others until he totally gives of himself to all others.

As musicians, we should give our art over to other persons. Art itself is alive, very similar to the person that makes it. In essence, when participating in the music-making process, you should strive to become selfless so that the art becomes the most important aspect of the performance. By doing this, one reveals, through music, the soulful, spiritual self. Another aspect of this kenotic act is that as a musician, you should strive to unmake your personality in front of people so that they become more. You become less so that others become more. Or, perhaps more accurately stated, you become less so that the music becomes more. In essence, a conductor's personality dwindles until the choir becomes real persons in front of an audience.

You become less so that the choir can become more.

If you can achieve this lessening of personality through the kenotic act, you will observe a very ordinary peacefulness, a sobriety of context within which music gains a strong and compelling voice. That sobriety of soulfulness may be the first truly soulful sobriety one has experienced since childhood. That sobriety of soul is the stillness that is so necessary to make music which compels one's life forward through inherent truth that exists within the music. It is that realized truth which gives the lived life profound meaning.

Access to Stillness

One must make time for stillness in one's life. Because so much of the world literally clamors for our undivided attention, we find ourselves constantly focusing toward the outside world, while we virtually ignore our own interiority and soul. The pace of the world and the pace of our lives almost predetermine that we will have no time in our lives to know ourselves. Consequently, many persons live their entire lives without ever really knowing themselves.

How does one access this stillness from which musical intuition speaks? That is your decision. It may be as simple as setting aside five to ten minutes each day for you to be quiet and to be with yourself so that you can hear yourself rather than others. It may be Yoga study. It may be time each day where you write whatever comes to mind in a journal. It may be the study of Tai Chi. It may be prayer, prayer that is made less with the head and more with the heart. Prayer can be as simple as being and just breathing in and out.

Whatever way you choose to explore stillness, it is necessary to do it. You must make time in your day, no matter how long, for time with yourself. Your ability to access stillness and understand calm will provide the music you conduct a new voice, a new sense of center and groundedness.

In light of the material of this chapter, now consider
1 Corinthians 13:

> If I have all the eloquence of men or of angels, but speak without love, I am simply a gong booming or a cymbal clashing. If I have the gift of prophecy, understanding all the mysteries there are, and knowing everything, and if I have faith in all its fullness, to move mountains, but without love, I am nothing at all.
>
> Love is always patient and kind; it is never jealous; love is never boastful or conceited; it is never rude or selfish; it

does not take offense, and is not resentful. Love takes no pleasure in other people's sins but delights in the truth; it is always ready to excuse, to trust, to hope, and to endure whatever comes.

Love does not come to an end. But if there are gifts of prophecy, the time will come when they must fail; or the gift of languages; it will not continue forever; and knowledge—for this, too, the time will come when it must fail. For our knowledge is imperfect and our prophesying is imperfect; but once perfection comes, all imperfect things disappear. When I was a child, I used to talk like a child, and think like a child, and argue like a child, but now I am a man, all childish ways are put behind me. Now we are seeing a dim reflection in a mirror; but we shall be seeing face to face. The knowledge that I have now is imperfect; but then I shall know as fully as I am known.

In short, there are three things that last: faith, hope and love; and the greatest of these is love.

I Corinthians 13

Suggested Reading and Sources

The audio tapes that accompany this text are designed to provide you with the beginning tools to access your own unique spirituality. For those of you who would like some guided direction as to how to "pray" and to access that stillness, I recommend that you read *Praying Body and Soul* edited by Gabriel Galkache. I also highly recommend that you examine *Sadhana: A Way to God* by Anthony deMello. A book that contains a wealth of thought on combines text and photographs is *When True Simplicity Is Gained* by Martin Marty and Micah Marty.

Finally, the reader is encouraged to read the postscript essay by Donald Sheehan in the rear portion of this text immediately after completing this chapter.

Chapter Nine
The Heart, Stillness, and Simplicity

We can respond from the heart, reawaken the heart. In the ancient world the organ of perception was the heart. The heart was immediately connected to things via the senses. The word for perception or sensation in Greek was aisthesis, which means at root a breathing in or taking in of the world, the gasp, "aha," the "uh" of the breath in wonder, shock, amazement, an aesthetic response to the image (eidolon) presented. In ancient Greek physiology and in biblical psychology the heart was the organ of sensation: it was also the place of imagination. The common sense (sensus communis) was lodged in and around the heart, and its role was to apprehend images. For Marsilion Ficino, too, the spirit in the heart received and transmitted the impression of the senses. The heart's function was aesthetic. (p. 107)

To move with the heart toward the world shifts psychotherapy from conceiving itself as a science to imagining itself more like an aesthetic activity. (p. 112)

James Hillman
The Thought of the Heart and Soul of the World

Question: What, in brief, is the power of the work of stillness?

Answer: Stillness mortifies the outward senses and resurrects the inward movements, whereas an outward manner of life does the opposite, that is, it resurrects the outward senses and deadens the inward movements. (p. 175)

A man who craves esteem cannot be rid of the causes of grief. (p. 5)

The more a man's tongue flees talkativeness, the more his intellect is illumined so as to be able to discern deep thoughts; for the rational intellect is bemuddled by talkativeness. (p. 86)

Be everyman's friend, but in your mind remain alone. (p. 247)

No man has understanding if he is not humble, and he who lacks humility is devoid of understanding. No man is humble if he is not peaceful, and he who is not peaceful is not humble. And no man is peaceful without rejoicing. (p. 247)

Silence is a mystery of the age to come, but words are instruments of this world. (p. 321)

Not every quiet man is humble, but every humble man is quiet. (p. 349)

Saint Issac the Syrian
The Ascetical Homilies of Saint Issac the Syrian

There is as much worship in good workmanship done in the right spirit, as in any other act; the spirit of the thing done and not the act itself is the key to tell whether anything done be worship or not, but God, the master workman, who has made the minutest insect with as much care as the mammoth elephant, sets us the example of good works. Imitation is the sincerest praise.

"The Shaker Manifesto" in
Thomas Moore, *The Education of the Heart*

Achieving Mimetic Balance

How does one achieve a spiritual balance in one's life? That is, how do you keep deepening within yourself, but still remain able to connect in a human way with the musicians who sit in front of you? In a previous chapter, a mimetic theory for musicians was detailed. Examine the words "Be," "Do," and "Have:" they can function as cues for achieving the right balances within one's life in order to allow spiritual growth and deepening to occur. While the Have and Do of life are important, it is critical not to overinvest in them. To do so causes one to assume an external importance that frequently, if not always, gets in the way of the music-making process. Your focus should be on Being. If one looks at the diagram on the next page, one can see the delicate balance that is necessary for this spiritual equilibrium to occur.

How does one correct the imbalance among Be, Do, and Have? Upon examining the diagram that follows, it is interesting to predict how those imbalances will affect the horizontal of the diagram. Assuming that one understands the effects of mimetic envy on the artist, one must strive to maintain a balance between the complicated issues in one's life (represented by the vertical elements) and the relationship between yourself and others (as represented by the horizontal). The intersection of the vertical and the horizontal can be considered to be what we refer to as the heart. That is, within the heart lives the total culmination of one's life work; in essence, the elements of Being and Doing contribute to what we have come to know as the heart.

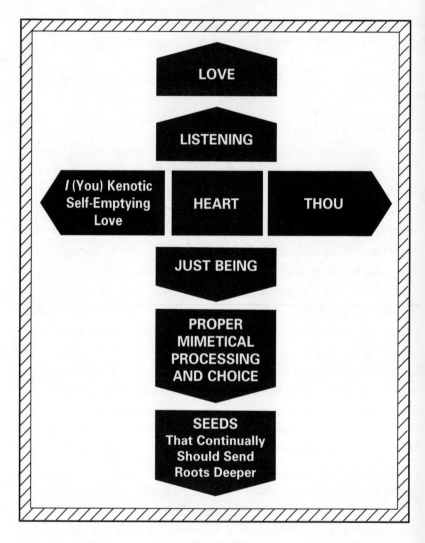

NOTE: All above is surrounded by shading that is representational of shedding. Shedding refers to those things in life that need to be cast off in order for us to arrive at a better understanding of us and what is at our very center. Things that are shed are those things throughout our life that pull us away from the center part of our being and cause us not to be connected to ourselves. Connection in this context denotes the ability to know ourselves.

The Horizontal Axis

If one looks at the diagram above, the horizontal axis is repre-
sentative of the constant interplay in the relationship with an
ensemble or group of persons. The vertical axis represents the
activities that cause one to be more aware of oneself, and hence
aware of others. The vertical axis represents the soulful activities of
the artist in daily life. The horizontal axis represents one's direct,
open, and vulnerable relationship with everyone involved in the
music-making process.

The two horizontal extremes between I and Thou are kept in
balance by the heart which is at the intersection of the vertical
soulful activities. Also, the relationship between self and others is
a function of the spiritual heart. The spiritual heart keeps the I and
Thou relationship in balance. I and Thou (the terms borrowed
from the writings of Martin Buber) place the person in a direct
and intimate relationship with others where both are on equal
ground as human beings despite their respective roles in the
music-making process. Both are and must be equal and constantly interactive, respectful, caring, and loving. I and Thou can only
function in a state of complete equilibrium brought about by
human relationships that are rooted in love, care, and selflessness.
I and Thou are equal. Musicians are equal. Human beings are
equal. When one end or the other (I or Thou) goes out of balance
because of a lack of human awareness for the other, the heart is
affected, and hence the music will be affected. The heart and one's
very inner being can only speak when all the elements of each I
and Thou are perceived because of the vulnerability of all parties
as equals in the music-making process. Without vulnerability
there can be no I, no Thou. Without vulnerability, each cannot
perceive the other's soul, so no connection between the I and the
Thou can take place. And without vulnerability, there is no chance
for self-emptying (kenotic) love to be shared through the music-
making process. It is wordless communication of the highest
order: soul to soul, spirit to spirit, using music as the vehicle. A

disconnection between I and Thou results in poor intonation, a lack of tone color, inconsistent tempo, and general instability within the music. But more importantly, that instability in the music is caused by a deep instability within the persons making music which occurs at the most profound and deep levels within them, almost unconsciously. That activity within one's soul is one of the marvels of the human condition.

The Vertical Axis: The Process of Deepening

Much of the activity within the soul is a direct result of soul-wrestling which must go on day in and day out. It is the work of living. The process of deepening in all its stages is represented by the elements below the horizontal axis. In taking this spiritual journey, you have already heard in this book how important it is to spend time to quiet the clatter of both life and cognitive mind so that one can begin to hear the voices within that define who one is. "Just being" is just that: being able to sit for considerable blocks of time and be with oneself. That quiet time allows one to begin to know oneself in order that one then can share oneself with others. One aspect of "just being" is making the right mimetical choices: consciously choosing love over anger; helping instead of hurting; loving oneself instead of engaging in self-mutilation; exhibiting on all occasions profound human care and love.

If one is able to consistently make the right mimetical choices, each choice can be considered to be a new "seed" in one's life experience. Every time a correct mimesis is created, another seed is planted. The planting of those seeds is an internal, deeply spiritual process, half achieved through conscious action, and half achieved through the work of "just being." The sowing of that seed and of all of the seeds within oneself is ultimately manifest in the music. The longer the seeds have been planted, the more they take root. The rooting can only take place when proper mimetical choices are constantly made at an almost blinding pace within the rehearsal and the performance. Continued correct mimetical choice causes the seed to take root and go even deeper. While many persons achieve certain aspects of this paradigm, many ultimately do not realize the fruits of their labors because they lack constant and consistent deepening within themselves. It is one's depth and overall interiority of soul which causes music to speak in the most compelling of ways. The music moves from the realm of replication of notes and rhythms and sound to directly speaking to the souls of all those who listen. The vulnerability of one or a group can cause vulnerability and opening in others. This opening and vulnerability is desperately needed in a world in which people do not deepen because they have been hurt. Vulnerability is total, unbiased acceptance. People do not deepen because they have not received from the world at large a care and human love that allows them to stay open and vulnerable. Their very lives, unbeknownst to them, are causing them not to be able to have a human relationship with others, and hence a relationship with the music. There can be no music without life. There is no life without soulful exploration and living. One's spiritual life is not so much a matter of faith, but a matter of practice: very repetitious practice and revisitation day in and day out. One's faith as an artist is not so much a matter of religious faith as it is a capacity for wonder. That soulful exploration and constant striving to understand a non-narcisstic love of self and others is central to the healthy life of the artist. To closely paraphrase St. Augustine, one cannot know Thee without knowing Thee (self). One must believe that the spirits and souls of composers speak through the written notes. The human spirit behind each musical idea can only be transmitted through those that are fully connected to their own soulfulness through deepening.

To be sure, deepening is a lifelong journey. But make no mistake about it: that journey of deepening can only be explored through understanding of self obtained at the same time that one strives for vulnerability and connection with other human beings, every minute of one's life. That is what being fully alive as an artist and a person really means.

Part Five

THE END AS THE BEGINNING

Chapter Ten
Soulwrestling: Awareness and Salvation for the Creative Artist

Wrestling is itself the synthesis of making love and making war. To wrestle with God is to make in human action and on the human level the same unification of the same opposites that God unifies. It is a way of bringing to visibility that paradoxical image of God which is stamped deep within us. For to wrestle with God is also to wrestle with human beings—ourselves and others. It is to face polarities and unify them. Not only to face the polarities of Same and Other when we face each other, but also within ourselves to face the polarities of fear and guilt, of love and anger—and to unify them. (p. 29)

Arthur Waskow
Godwrestling—Round 2

The claim that good teaching comes from the identity and integrity of the teacher might sound like a truism, and a pious one at that: good teaching comes from good people.

But by identity and integrity I do not mean only our noble features, or the good deeds we do, or the brave faces we wear to conceal our confusions and complexi-

ties. Identity and integrity have as much to do with our
shadows and limits, our wounds and fears, as with our
strengths and potentials (p. 13).

How does one attend to the voice of the teacher
(musician) within? I have no particular methods to suggest, other than the familiar bones: solitude and silence,
meditative reading and walking in the woods, keeping a
journal, finding a friend who will listen. I simply propose
that we need to learn as many ways as we can of "talking
to ourselves."

That phrase, of course, is one we normally use to name a
symptom of mental imbalance—a clear sign of how
culture regards the idea of the inner voice! But people
who learn to talk to themselves may soon delight in the
discovery that the teacher within is the sanest conversation partner they have ever had. (p. 32)

Parker J. Palmer
The Courage to Teach

The beginning of awe is wonder, and the beginning of
wisdom is awe. (p. 52)

Abraham Joshua Heschel
Between God and Man

Your vocation is the place where your deep gladness
and the world's deep hunger meet. (p. 119)

Frederick Buechner
Wishful Thinking

"Mitch, you asked about caring for people you don't
even know. But can I tell you the thing I'm learning with
this disease?"

"What's that?"

"The most important thing in life is to learn how to give out love, and to let it come in."

His voice dropped to a whisper. "Let it come in. We think we don't deserve love, we think if we let it in we'll become too soft. But a wise man named Levine said it right. He said, 'Love is the only rational act.'"

He repeated it carefully, pausing for effect. "Love is the only rational act." (p. 52)

Mitch Albom
Tuesdays with Morrie

Man is our chief problem. His physical and mental reality is beyond dispute; his meaning, his spiritual relevance is a question that cries for an answer. Is it not right to suggest that the agony of contemporary man is the agony of a spiritually stunted man? The image of man is larger than the frame into which he was contracted; we have underestimated the nature of man. Even the form in which we ask the question about man is biased by our own conception of man as a thing. We ask: What is man? Yet the true question should be: Who is man? As a thing man is explicable; as a person he is both a mystery and a surprise. As a thing he is finite; as a person he is inexhaustible. (p. 27)

Man is not only a special kind of being. His being human depends upon certain relations without which he ceases to be human. The decision to give priority to the question what is human about being a human being is based upon the assumption that the category of human is not simply derived from the category of being. The attribute "human" in the term of "human being" is not an accidental quality, added to the essence of his being. It is his essence. Human being demands being human. An analysis of the human situation discloses a number of essential modes of being human.

It is indeed conceivable that man may continue to be without being human. Human being and being human are both exposed to danger, the latter even more than the former. "Being human" must always be rescued from chaos or extinction. (p. 29)

Ultimate self-penetration is neither possible nor desirable. What we may aim at is a degree of self-understanding which would enable us to project our living rather than let our living be a projection of the crowd, a fashion or a whim. Our task must include the effort to discern and to disclose the authentic as well as the unauthentic prepossessions, the honest as well as dishonest manifestations of inner life. (p. 31)

Remember that there is meaning beyond absurdity. Know that every deed counts, that every word is power....Above all, remember that you must build your life as if it were a work of art....(p. ix)

Abraham Joshua Heschel
I Asked for Wonder

When the deepest part of you becomes engaged in what you are doing, when your activities and actions become gratifying and purposeful, when what you do serves both yourself and others, when you do not tire within but seek the sweet satisfaction of your life and your work, you are doing what you were meant to be doing. The personality that is engaged in the work of its soul is buoyant. It is not burdened with negativity. It does not fear. It experiences purposefulness and meaning. It delights in its work and in others. It is fulfilled and fulfilling. (p. 236)

Gary Zukav
The Seat of the Soul

Art is an articulator of the soul's uncensored purpose
and deepest will. (p. 122)

> Shaun McNiff in
> Gregg Levoy, *Callings*

I have not spoken of the role of love in its everyday
manifestations. If one is going to speak of great art as
"evidence," is not ordinary human love an even more
striking evidence of a transcendent principle of good?
Plato was prepared to take it as a starting point. (There
are several starting points.) One cannot but agree that in
some sense this is the most important thing of all; and
yet human love is normally too profoundly possessive
and also too "mechanical" to be a place of vision. There is
a paradox here about the nature of love itself. That the
highest love is in some sense impersonal is something
which we can indeed see in art, but which I think we
cannot see clearly, except in a very piecemeal manner, in
the relationships of human beings. Once again, the place
of art is unique. The image of the Good as a transcendent magnetic centre seems to me the least corruptible
and most realistic picture for us to use in our reflections
upon the moral life. (p. 75)

> Iris Murdoch
> *The Sovereignty of Good*

In truth, without afflictions there is no life. (p. 294)

> Saint Issac the Syrian
> *The Ascetical Homilies of Saint Issac the Syrian*

Rather than a soul in a body, become a body in a soul.
Reach for your soul. Reach even farther. The impulse of
creation and power authentic—the hourglass point
between energy and matter: that is the seat of the soul.

What does it mean to touch that place? (p. 248)

Gary Zukav
The Seat of the Soul

Awe is an intuition for the dignity of all things, a realiza-
tion that things not only are what they are but also stand,
however remotely, for something supreme.

Awe is a sense for the transcendence, for the reference
everywhere to the mystery beyond all things. It enables
us to perceive in the world intimations of the divine...to
sense the ultimate in the common and the simple; to feel
in the rush of the passing stillness of the eternal. (p. 9)

Abraham Joshua Heschel
I Asked for Wonder

It would seem clear that no one can call upon Thee
without knowing thee.

Saint Augustine of Hippo

So in the end, all of this may be a curse in some ways. If you are
passionate, alive, and committed to your music making, the
awareness of even one idea in this book will cause you to wrestle
with yourself endlessly. Day in and day out, you will struggle within yourself to know yourself. So be it. The task of an artist,
whether you be a conductor, a recital singer, or a choir member at
church, is to understand that your music is what you are, or who
you know yourself to be. Constant visitations with oneself
through stillness times can bring clarity to your vision. Making
the conscious choice over and over again to care and love yourself
and others is the energy by which the spiritual journey can be
made.

If you choose to make the journey as suggested in this book,
know that your journey will be unique because your life and spirit are unique. My journey will differ greatly from yours because

our lives are different. But where we ultimately "live"— in our souls—is identical for all of us. Hopefully you will find that if you work on any of the concepts presented in this book, your music making will take on a new and exciting life. Within the rehearsal room or studio you will know yourself the best. Love, care, and compassion will begin to abound.

The problem becomes more complicated when one tries to carry what was learned via the music into your daily life. I remarked to a very good Catholic priest friend that I cannot understand why I can be so patient, caring, and loving with my choir and yet not demonstrate those qualities in the world outside of music. I remarked that the other morning I raised my voice at my daughter because she didn't have her shoes on to go to school. Here is the person who I love most in the entire world, and I have no patience with her. My priest friend remarked, "Because it is not about the shoes."

He is right. It is not about the shoes. It is about all of the issues I have yet to ponder, make no mistake about it. By the way, people have been struggling with these issues for thousands of years. Writing in the last years of the fourth century A.D., Saint Augustine of Hippo describes his own spiritual awakening in *The Confessions* not by recounting the events of his life, but by affirming the human search for transcendence. In his writings, one discovers through the pain and examination of his own life that the ultimate truth was not God's, but rather his own. It is an accurate account of his heartfelt longings. Sage advice for an artist.

One can also look at the Psalms for more history of the search for soul.

> Hide not thy face from me in the day when I am in trouble;
> incline thine ear unto me; in the day when I call answer me speedily.
> For my days are consumed like smoke, and my bones are burned as an hearth.

> My heart is smitten, and withered like grass; so that I
>   forget to eat my bread.
> By reason of the voice of my groaning my bones
>   cleave to my skin.
> I am like a pelican of the wilderness: I am like an owl
>   of the desert.
> I watch, and am as a sparrow alone upon the house
>   top.
> Mine enemies reproach me all the day; and they that
>   are mad against me, are sworn against me.
> For I have eaten ashes like bread, and mingled my
>   drink with weeping.
> Because of thine indignation and thy wrath: for thou
>   has lifted me up and cast me down.
> My days are like a shadow that declineth; and I am
>   withered like grass.
>
>   Psalm 102
>   King James Bible

Even a cursory reading of the Psalms will detail an almost schizophrenic view into the human spirit—a view into the many questions that search and painfully probe for the true nature of human existence. In essence, it is the search for soulfulness amidst the muck of life.

In our own time soulful writing is in abundance. For some reason, the twentieth century has been witness to some of the most inhumane acts experienced in the past two millennia. The First World War, the Holocaust, and other horrific events have yielded up poetry and writing that document those authors' own spiritual journeys in the face of annihilation. They are essays in hope, love, and care. They are essays of people who were put on a journey and as a result were thrust by life's events to understand their very souls. Such is the stuff of real living.

To be a musician is a precious gift. Through our art, we can learn who we are, and where we live. By making the journey ourselves, we can help others along the way and help them live more complete lives through the music they sing or play. We can also become blessed with the awareness that music grows out of the spirits that create it. If we listen profoundly to the music we make, it is the sound of that music that will lead us through our personal journey.

If you are now expecting a summary, there is none. That summary can only be written by you. That summary can only be product of the journey that you will either choose to take or avoid out of fear.

Hopefully, you will choose the former. The struggle will be painful, but so rewarding. I am thankful that I was started on my journey by Elaine Brown and guided carefully and lovingly by the choirs I conduct. It will be your ongoing journey that will transform your art and make your art reflect real living. Real soulfulness is one's ability to be open to any possibility. Soulfulness is when our inner matches our outer; an integration. Such is the stuff of great music.

> Let our gardening hands be gentle ones.
> Let us not root up one another's ideas before they have time to bloom.
> Let us bear with the process of growth, dormancy, cyclicality, fruition, and reseeding.
> Let us never be hasty to judge, reckless in our urgency to force unnatural growth.
> Let there be, always, a place for the artist toddler to try, to falter, to fail and to try again.
> Let us remember that in nature's world every loss has meaning.
> The same is true for us.
> Turned to good use, a creative failure must be the compost that nourishes next season's creative success.
> Remember, we are in this for the long haul, the ripening and harvest, not the quick fix.

Art is an act of the soul: ours is a spiritual community.
                                          Julia Cameron
                                          The Artist's Way

Home is where one starts from. As we grow older
The world becomes stranger, the pattern more
    complicated
Of dead and living. Not the intense moment
And not the lifetime of one man only
But of old stones that cannot be deciphered.
There is a time for the evening under starlight,
A time for the evening under lamplight
(The evening with the photograph album).
Love is most nearly itself
Where here and now cease to matter.
Old men ought to be explorers
Here and there does not matter.
We must be still and still moving
Into another intensity
For a further union, a deeper communion
Through the dark cold and the empty desolation,
The wave cry, the wind cry, the vast waters
Of the petrel and the porpoise. In my end is my
    beginning.

                                          T. S. Elliot
                                          Four Quartets

POSTSCRIPT ESSAYS

From the Author

It was my desire from the outset of this book to have some other persons contribute short essays concerning their experiences with the content of this book. There were no guidelines given. Yet, what emerged are three different, but similar, essays that help further illuminate the book. Each, in their own way has grappled with the issues in this book. In all cases they have been my teachers and friends, too. It is an honor to have them contribute to this work.

Postscript Essays

The Musicians Soul:
A Graduate Student Reflects
by Matthew Mehaffey

All students have expectations when they enter an educational environment. When I started my Master's Degree in Choral Conducting at Westminster Choir College I had expectations about what I would be learning. I knew I would have ear training and conducting classes. I would learn more about the human voice and how to run a rehearsal. The university had all my requirements clearly laid out in the course catalog; there seemed to be no surprises. I knew exactly what to expect.

During the first few months of graduate school all of my preconceived notions proved to be true. I was being well educated in all the technical aspects of being a choral conductor. My classes proved challenging, but I was prepared to work. Practice began to make perfect; I was off to a good start as a graduate student.

I remember feeling pleased with my progress and my technical improvement during the first few months of school. I was learning, I liked my classes and classmates, and my teachers were knowledgeable and inspiring. I was making friends at my new school. Consequently my spirits were high. School was not going to be so tough. I was coasting through my master's degree, completely unaware of the pending storm.

Midway through my first semester a few of my teachers confronted me about my progress. All of them said I was doing fine work but I was not quite reaching my musical potential. In a zealous way I was flattered by these statements. Clearly these professors thought I was making progress, and obviously they recognized potential in my musical ability. Maybe they wanted me to work harder? I could do that! But at the same time I felt threatened by what they said. The overtones of our conversations revealed they were not pleased with my work; I could and should be doing better.

I thought about my professors' advice a great deal. I wanted to do better, but felt I was doing just fine. I could tell I was learning and progressing, so what could be the problem my professors had with me? I did not understand what they wanted. I needed one of my professors to tell me what I needed to do. After all, professors had always given me the answers I needed before. If I needed to know how to fix intonation problems in the tenor section, they could give me countless remedies. If I needed to know about Baroque performance practice, I could get a plethora of responses. To my surprise, when I finally asked them what I needed to do to expedite my progress, they failed to give a definite answer. They all responded by saying I had to figure that out for myself. They said all my skills were in place and I had learned all my musical lessons well. Then they dropped the bomb. They explained to me that I was learning a great deal about music but I wasn't learning anything about myself. They continued pressing, "How can you produce honest music if you aren't being true to yourself first?" And if that wasn't enough, "Do you know who you are? Do you like yourself?" At first I kind of laughed at the idea that I did not know myself or didn't like myself. I had been living with myself every day for twenty-two years, so of course I knew who I was. I was a happy person and had always been popular, so naturally I liked myself. I took the advice with a grain of salt, put the idea in the back of my head, and continued my master's program.

Not much time passed before I hit a serious musical roadblock. My musical progress came to standstill. I continued to learn but did not progress. My brain took in all the information presented in the classroom, but I failed to apply my new knowledge when it came to actual music making. I had come to a crossroads I didn't know how to cross. My conducting continued to be technically proficient, but I gradually became more and more detached from the music. I started to hate school. I enjoyed my classes and all I was learning, but I grew very frustrated with myself and with my inability to progress to a higher level. I started to envy many of my classmates' abilities and the connections they were able to make and maintain with the music. Why could I not get there like they could? I knew I possessed this ability, but I could not find it. Soon I started doubting myself. After the doubt came, my conducting suffered dramatically. I cannot point to a specific instance when this doubt and self-mutilation commenced, but nevertheless, it had begun: I was caught in a cycle of self-mutilation.

It didn't take long for my self-doubt to manifest itself in every aspect of my musical life. Soon my sight-singing skills suffered, my singing lacked its usual confidence, and my teaching was tentative and uninspiring. I had no desire to practice or study. I was in a real rut. The doubt spread like a cancer into the rest of my life. I started feeling self-conscious, wondering if people liked me. I began to dislike myself.

Within six months of entering graduate school I went from being a confident young student with a willingness to learn and grow to a confused student who had lost complete respect for himself as a musician (and was rapidly losing interest in himself as a person). I was dangerously close to failure.

I know all of this sounds very melodramatic, and maybe it is to some extent, but I honestly hit bottom. I was not clinically depressed or on medication and I did not ponder suicide or anything crazy like that, but for the first time in my life I was confronted with the possibility of failing. I was not becoming a better musician. There was too much "personal stuff" getting in the way.

I had to do something.

With the help of a few of my professors I began a journey into myself. Again this was not something they could make me do, *I* had to make the decision to take the journey into my own life. I started slowly, scared of what I might find. I spent time alone with myself every day, I read some books and went places alone. I started writing down my personal thoughts and concerns. I soon found externalizing my thoughts helped me stop dwelling on my musical problems. It also helped me solve my daily problems with increased clarity. I was meeting myself for the first time.

After I felt "introduced to myself" I went to work on my musical problems, particularly my newfound lack of self-confidence. Where did my self-doubt come from? It seemed to me that I had always been a positive, confident person. Why then did I let myself get to a point where I could not function as a musician? I could not discern why I was in a rut. Where did my positive outlook go?

After weeks of intense searching and wrestling I came up with the "small fish/big pond" hypothesis. I realized that up until my entrance into graduate school I had always been a musical leader—the big fish in a small pond. Now I was just one of the many talented conducting students. I was not accustomed to being surrounded by people of superior talent. To a twenty-two year old this is a pretty serious awakening. After grappling with this reality I said to myself, "OK, there are other talented people in the world, this should not come as a surprise. But why does their existence make me any less of a musician or person?" Seems like a simple question, but I soon found it was not quite so easy to answer. I started thinking again, and after several more weeks of intense self-deliberation I came to a profoundly simple conclusion: "It doesn't."

It is amazing to me that it took so much "spiritual wrestling" to arrive at such a simple solution. I had been too concerned with the progress of others and rating how their abilities compared to mine, instead of realizing the only way to improve my musicianship was to believe in myself. Strangely enough I realized that I actually knew myself the entire time. I had been so caught up in doubt that I had forgotten who I was. This experience did not make me feel like a completely different person; I merely felt affirmed and renewed. I was my old self again. My own psyche led down a path of doubt. By deepening I found a new source of power and a new passion for music. I was on the way out of the depths.

At this point I tried to apply the mimetical principles mentioned in this book. I made a conscious decision to trust myself more and to care for myself more. Not in an egotistical way, but in way that would allow me to grow and to nurture my creative process. This did not turn out to be a one-time decision. I literally make it hundreds of times per day. I know if I don't make this decision every time I come to a roadblock, no matter how minor, I will default to my habit of self-mutilation.

From the moment I began making this decision my creative productivity increased profoundly. I felt alive and confident. I now love to do what I do. This is not to say I never have a bad day or that I never doubt myself, but now I have ways to cope with the inevitable crossroads. Instead of dwelling on what I can't do or what I do wrong, I continually remind myself of my strengths and work to improve my shortcomings. I find it helpful to approach my weaknesses without losing sight of my strengths, because ultimately I know it will be my strengths that overcome the weaknesses. Now when I get into a jam in a rehearsal I stay behind myself and maintain my confidence, and invariably I can solve the problem. In the past I would have done one of several things: 1) blamed myself for my inability; 2) externalized my anger and fear on the choir by yelling at them to watch me, or sit up (something completely unrelated to the music); or 3) completely avoided the problem and said, "I'll come back to that." None of these options in any way leads to a successful musical experience. When I think of how I used to treat myself and others I literally get scared. My actions were far from humane, they were destructive.

I continued to spend time with myself over the summer after my first year in graduate school. I grappled with ideas of trust and self-worth and started to really believe in myself. I did a great deal of teaching in the summer time. I worked with a great group of high school students. Teaching them was one of the most educating experiences I have ever had. It was very clear that they believed in me and in what I was teaching them.

Once my second year began I was determined to stay in a positive frame of mind. I was not going to take the road I had the year before. The first few months were wonderful and then I was tested. My friends and I had formed a small choir to sing at a theological conference in New Hampshire. The conductor of this ensemble was a firm believer in the mimetical ideas discussed in the book. We had several rehearsals to prepare for this concert, and the choir was singing wonderfully. We were very excited to make the trip to New Hampshire. The day before we left we discovered the conductor would not be able to join us because of unfortunate circumstances. We were all very disappointed because we were intent on singing at this festival. After a night of heated debate the fifteen of us decided we would attempt to sing the concert without a conductor. We were off to New Hampshire.

Upon arrival we started our dress rehearsal. The rehearsal did not go well. After the first mistake the doubt started and we all felt nervous, even scared. As we continued to rehearse each piece got worse and worse. Finally one of the women in the group externalized her fear and frustration by saying, "This is just not working." By this point I could feel the tension in the room. I knew that if I did not say something we would never be able to sing the concert. I spoke up. I challenged the group to believe in themselves, to trust each other, and to trust in the music. I felt uncomfortable talking to my peers about these issues, but to my surprise they all listened to what I had to say. I finally said, "We all need to sit here in silence and think about what it is we have to do." So we sat. And sat. We thought to ourselves and looked at each other. There was an incredible gathering of strength in our silent time. After approximately ten minutes of silence one of the students offered a prayer. Others offered words of encouragement. The mood of the room started to change. We all knew that it was time to sing.

We started our "new rehearsal" by singing Palestrina's *Sicut Cervus*. Immediately we all realized our sound had changed profoundly. I will never forget this run-through of this piece. We were alive and open. We were now reacting to each other as musicians but more importantly as human beings. After hearing our new sound we all knew everything was going to be all right. We were inspired to work harder.

We stayed connected to each other for the rest of the rehearsal and through dinner and the concert. The concert ended up being a wonderful success. It was by no means perfect, but that was okay because the fifteen of us became a community that night. We received so many wonderful comments from the rather large audience, saying they had never heard singing like that before. I am convinced our singing was a product of our spirits. Our openness invited our audience to see who we were. We sang as human beings who cared for the beauty of our art, not as snobbish musicians intent on impressing an audience.

After the concert we all knew we had just been part of something incredibly special. As a group we talked about how our fears and doubts almost prevented us from being a part of such a wonderful experience. For a short amount of time we were all able to rid ourselves of our everyday problems and believe in our true selves. Remarkably we all believed in each other, making ourselves very open and vulnerable so we could find the music inside of us. We found music and truth that a textbook could write about, but not make us experience. We all knew connection between ourselves could improve our music, we just never understood how profoundly. I feel I can speak for my peers by saying we learned more about ourselves, our humanity, and music that night than ever before.

When I arrived back from this trip I continued with my exploration. I wanted so badly to relive that experience. It was so invigorating. I was proud of what my friends and I accomplished. I was so glad we did not give up on ourselves and I was happy that I recognized when the group needed to stop doubting themselves.

After this experience I realized that I had passed the crossroads I had come to. The trip to New Hampshire served as my defining moment in my spiritual struggle. If I had not been wrestling with ideas of trust and belief I never would have had the courage to experience what I did in New Hampshire.

Being connected to myself and to my friends enabled me to deeply connect with music for the first time. It is ironic how it took adversity for me to find such a simple calm place. This time I am proud to say the adversity did not scare me. I was calm and collected. I had the presence of mind to believe in the talents I possess. My friends and I who were in this small group are not necessarily the best musicians in our school, but we made music that night like I had never heard before. I firmly believe our music was a function of who we were as people. That night music was made by individuals who cared for the common goal of beauty, and for each other. Not a mean word was said that weekend. We were all beautiful human beings. We will all remember that weekend for the rest of our lives. I know that no matter what I do for the rest of my life I will have this experience to remind me that music, trust, and honesty really do exist.

I realize this essay makes it sound like I have found all the answers. Believe me, I know I haven't. I just cleared the first hurdle. I have awakened to a whole new way of existing. My way of life has changed, but I am still me. I accept that I do not have all "the answers." Prior to my awareness this would have disturbed me greatly. Now I wonder, how can I have an answer before I hear the question? With each challenge I am faced with from now on I know I must listen to the question. Then I must listen to myself to find *my* answer. (This may not be the answer for somebody else.) I am ready to meet these challenges. I only wish someone told me this would be expected of me when I entered graduate school. I must have missed that page in the course catalog.

Matthew Mehaffey holds a Bachelor's of Music in Music Education from Bucknell University and a Master's with distinction in Choral Conducting from Westminster Choir College of Rider University. He has studied conducting with noted conductors William Payn, James Jordan, Volker Hempfling, and Joseph Flummerfelt. While at Westminster Mehaffey was the Assistant Conductor to the Westminster Chapel Choir, and participated in many discussions regarding this publication with author and conductor James Jordan. He is currently pursuing a DMA in Choral Conducting from the University of Arizona under the tutelage of Maurice Skones.

Postscript Essays

The Musician's Soul:
New Journey

... we need to be willing to let our intuition guide us,
and then be willing to follow that guidance directly and
fearlessly.

Shakti Gawain

I'm not sure whether it was an act of courage or lunacy. Why, in my eleventh year of a highly successful career, did I decide to "ditch it all," sell everything I owned, leave my family and friends behind, and step out into the "great unknown"? Why else, but for music. What I didn't know then was that the answers to my questions could not and would not be resolved by magically completing a Master's degree... and so the journey continues.

In the summer of 1994 I came to Westminster Choir College to study summer session courses in conducting, voice building, and rehearsal techniques. At this point in my career I had achieved the goal of building a high-quality choral program at the high school level and was extremely proud of the "statistics" that garnered my success. But despite attending every conducting workshop possible with people I respected and admired, I knew I had reached the limit of the resources available to me in Australia, so it was on the advice of a colleague who had lived and studied in the USA that I embarked on my journey to Princeton. Little did I or anyone else realize the impact this trip would have. In fact, on reflection, the sequence of events that allowed me to finally make the return journey to Westminster in August 1996 were nothing short of remarkable. To make a long story short, I was honored to receive a prestigious Rotary Foundation Ambassadorial Scholarship that provided significantly for my first year of study. Once accepted to Westminster in April 1996, the enormity of my decision started to hit, although it was not until I was 30,000 feet above the Pacific and on my way to the USA that I realized there was no turning back. Buoyed by enthusiastic optimism and the unwavering support of family, colleagues, and friends, thus began my new life—my great American adventure!

There were many different experiences—some predictable and many unexpected. Adjusting to living in a foreign country was initially much harder than I had anticipated, and there were some big problems that I hadn't counted on, such as my husband being sent back to Australia for an "undetermined" period of time while the government corrected my visa status. But despite this and many other setbacks, the music at Westminster was wonderful, my new friends supportive, and I realized that I'd come too far to give up and run home at the first sign of trouble. Indeed, during the early months, it was the music that sustained me. It was quite overwhelming to be in the Westminster environment, surrounded by strangers who were also drawn there by the mystical allure of the "Westminster way" as I had heard it referred to by others.

Fairly quickly I discovered that the study of choral conducting and the pursuit of making beautiful choral music at Westminster was not confined to accuracy of technique alone. My learning curve was steep indeed. Of course there was the published curriculum, but no-one told me about the "hidden" curriculum— the one that required me to "go deeper" or "let go" or "stay centered." Singing in Westminster Choir and Westminster Symphonic Choir rehearsals daily, and working with the Westminster Chapel Choir as the graduate assistant every day for two years was my idea of heaven, until I had to face myself, my inner-most fears, my self-doubt, my insecurities, and my secure old habit of self-mutilation. Why? Because of the music. Because I couldn't make music until I dealt with myself. You see, I had it all so neatly worked out. Work hard and practice constantly and all would be well! Or would it?

Even now I find it extremely difficult to explain the "transformations" in my being as a result of my Westminster experiences, and I use the plural deliberately, because I was blessed to be nurtured by numerous professors who took a particular interest in my music and development, and experienced many wonderful musical and life-changing events. In the first instance I had to learn to value my gut reactions or instincts. After many years of successfully burying myself and using the sheer force of my will to get a sound, I was now in a situation where I was simply told: "...you can run, but you can't hide. Every time you get up on the podium the choir senses where you are. You have to be centered and grounded or you'll never get them to sing!" I will never forget the sound the Chapel Choir made one October day—it was the hardest, most edgy sound I had ever heard and it totally frightened me. "What the hell was that?" I asked myself. At first I wanted to blame the choir. Surely it couldn't have been anything I was doing... you know I'd been making beautiful music with "my own choir" for years... but it was me, every last grating overtone was a product of my core, and that was the day I realized how connected the sound was to the emotional turmoil in my life, and how disconnected I was with myself. I was living alone, my closest friend and surrogate sister in America was suffering with a cancer relapse, I was trying to "fit-in" to the local scene, I was desperately homesick... and I was trying to kid myself that I could make beautiful music! How could I when I had not faced the fact that any of these issues were affecting my spirit, and by association my ability to function as a musician?

Looking back on that day (the day I momentarily contemplated hitting the streets and finding another way to make a living) I realize now that it was a gift and the beginning of what I now call my journey. Of course, the Westminster graduate journey progressed steadily, with many ups and downs along the way. What was remarkable about those years was the emphasis on "process" and the infinite patience and wisdom of my professors. How humbling it was, at my graduate choral conducting recital, to stand in front of two choirs comprising some of the most talented and generous musicians in the world, and realize that they were freely sharing their spirits and souls with me. It was a revelation: the moment that clarified and confirmed my understanding that I could trust my instincts, that I could believe in myself, and that my honesty and humanity are wonderful and powerful forces. That was my Westminster legacy.

It was not until I returned to Australia after two years away that I was able to put some distance and perspective on my Westminster experiences, and it was then that I realized how much being a foreigner had figured in my difficulties at times. On the one hand it was fun to be the campus novelty, coming from a country that held great appeal for literally every American I met, and of course, the accent was a source of much interest too. On the other hand, it mattered not how much I tried, American culture was so different from my own in every respect (often mysteriously so) and although I tried to blend in, the sense that I was different fed my insecurities. I think too that the Australian "tall poppy" syndrome, where every tall poppy tends to be chopped to size, was a negative influence, along with the sense that I was from a country of inferior cultural heritage. Certainly I did not have the up-front confidence in myself that many of my colleagues had, and at times I was quite appalled by the over-confidence of some of the average musicians I met who were pushing their way to the top.

Now I see how pointless my so-called modesty or humility really was. It was more a defense or an excuse that I used to protect myself, and it stopped me from achieving my potential, that is, until I decided to tackle it head-on! Now I am comfortable celebrating my uniqueness and my own experiences, although it was difficult when my perception of the Americans I was interacting with was heavily influenced by their own culture and country's artistic heritage. That I felt compelled to somehow try and absorb this if I was to be successful in the USA was not a bad thing in and of itself. But when taken to the extreme and used as a defense mechanism, then that's another story. It probably seems strange to you that in the field of music, the universal language, one would find this to be so, particularly in a country as ethnically diverse as the USA. However, this was my experience and I know of other international students who have had very similar experiences. Fortunately now I have the confidence to be comfortable with my "foreignness" and I am finding many wonderful opportunities to enjoy and utilize my unique perspective.

As I write these words I am amazed and humbled by the opportunities that have come my way since I graduated. I have the privilege of making beautiful music on a daily basis with students who are passionate about music, and in an environment where humanity is the driving force behind our music making. My journey continues, and so too does my struggle with my ability to curb my mimetic default of self-mutilation at the first sign of trouble. I have come to understand and accept that the journey of self-discovery is a life-long process and that my instincts are good. I continue to believe, most strongly, that my life, and by association my music, will be enriched by my ability to face adversity with courage—to face it head-on and turn it to my advantage so that all of my experiences, good and bad, become growth opportunities within the rich fabric of life. I'm convinced, more than ever, that I can dare to dream! I am excited and humbled by the tremendous responsibility of the blessings that are part-and-parcel of my work at Westminster. And so my journey of self-discovery continues... I believe that it is the interaction of the spiritual, emotional, intellectual, and creative forces that primarily shape our being and our ability to make music. To make beautiful music is a profound honor and an opportunity denied to those who are unable to search deep within themselves and honestly probe the depths of their hopes, their fears, and their insecurities.

Thus it is from a place deep within the self, the soul, wherein humility, honesty, and love are profoundly intertwined, that I know I can I find true meaning in the music, and evoke beautiful, musical responses from my choir. How do I know it's possible? Because it happens when I trust my singers and myself. It's like walking a tightrope every time I conduct—but I wouldn't have it any other way! Sure the risks are greater, but so is the outcome.

> We will discover the nature of our particular genius when we stop trying to conform to our own or to other peoples' models, learn to be ourselves, and allow our natural channel to open.
>
> Every time you don't follow your inner guidance, you feel a loss of energy, loss of power, a sense of spiritual deadness.
>
> Shakti Gawain

Heather J. Buchanan is assistant professor of conducting and assistant to the artistic director at Westminster Choir College of Rider University. She conducts the sophomore choir, Westminster Schola Cantorum, and also manages the Westminster Choir and the Westminster Symphonic Choir. Born in Brisbane, Australia, Ms. Buchanan graduated from the Queensland Conservatorium of Music (Australia) and has been a music educator and choral director for 13 years. She earned her Master of Music degree with distinction from Westminster, where she pursued a double major in choral conducting and music education. Ms. Buchanan also adjudicates competitions and works as a guest conductor and clinician at school and community choral festivals in Australia and on the east coast of the United States.

Postscript Essays

Shakespeare, Saint Isaac the Syrian, and the Choral Experience of Envy
by Donald Sheehan

Every choral singer knows the experience. In the making of choral art, the conductor inevitably seems to possess all the decisive power. The singer's relation to that power (as the conductor's) is always complex and sometimes disastrous. It is complex because the conductor is the center of the attentive gaze of singers who look to him—with an intensity little short of spellbound—to release their art. He literally holds their art in his hands and therefore not only possesses a centrality—and an apparent glory—that the singers do not, but actually has in his possession that which is their own. Yet without him, the fullness of their art is forever unrealized, as, without the singers, the conductor's art, too, is merely potential.

So the relation is complex and reciprocal. Each seems to hold (and often to withhold) the glory of the other. Indeed, this is not peculiar to choruses; it is the human condition. It brings to mind a line in a prayer: "Grant me a share in Thy glory." And it recalls the tragedy of Genesis where glory, shared with humankind in free abundance, yet appeared to be withheld and so was grasped: A share in God's glory was not enough; humanity needed to be *like* God. And so the disaster possible in all human relationships, and especially in choruses, opens up. We want to be *like* the ones who seem to possess the glory we feel is rightfully ours—and, even though we may admire them intensely, we want them *not* to be like that, *not* to have the glory: that is, we want to seize the glory and to eliminate our rival.

In the choral experience, as in life, one singer's desire for musical glory fuels the desire of every other—and thereby intensifies everyone's desire. Such reciprocal intensification exhibits that definitive quality of all desire termed by René Girard *mimetic* or *imitative*. Mimetic desire is therefore best understood as contagious. And precisely as does bacterial infection, the contagion of desire intensifies (rather than weakens) as it jumps swiftly, invisibly, and completely from one person to another. In a choir, the spiritual end result is exactly described by a choral singer who recently said of the choir, "I have an image of a crowd all scratching and scrambling across each other to get celebrity, mortally wounding each other in the process." Such are the dynamics of the mimetic disaster.

And here lies the conductor's most terrible power. The more she desires glory for herself, the more her singers will desire it for themselves, vying for her recognition and attention (as if to recapture from her the power they had initially bestowed upon her) and clawing each other for the prestige of solo parts, sometimes even seeking for weaknesses in the conductor that might open a way for dethronement, or at least for contempt. Comparably, the conductor escalates the dynamics of envy by endlessly consuming her singers' hungry rivalry for the favors she can bestow and the art she makes manifest in them. The result, for the conductor, is an insatiable appetite for her choir's envious gaze, an appetite properly seen as an addiction. There is, of course, an energy and intensity in all of this that will generate a certain musical excitement. But mimetic excitement will not finally make genuine music, for it is founded on a disintegrative and hence disharmonious process.

Envy is, above all, a spiritual affliction. It is not a psychologi-

cal condition—although it assuredly generates a storm of emotional effects in the afflicted. Nor is it an artistic activity—although
it sustains an endless critique of other people's artistic practices and
a ceaseless defense of one's own. The simplest statement of the
affliction is this: Envy believes that it will walk better if its neigh-
bor breaks his leg. Envy desires to have the beauty or power or talent that another possesses precisely because that other strongly and
gracefully possesses it, and it desires this at the other's expense.

Like all spiritual affliction, the choral experience of envy
almost always has a perfect cover-story: the singer is showing
"respect" for the conductor's great skill, and the conductor is seeking a strong performance "for the audience," or "to honor the
music." Such cover-stories camouflage and keep silent the opera-
tions of envy, for in such hushed hiddenness lies most of its power
to persist in its disintegrative work.

One of the deepest diagnoses of envy's mimetic turmoil is
Shakespeare's play *Troilus and Cressida*. In this play, Shakespeare
attempts to think through in dramatic terms all the ways wherein
envious desire actually—and terribly—works. At one crucial
point, the character Ulysses says this:

> . . . no man is lord of anything,
> Though in and of him there is much consisting,
> Till he communicates his parts to others;
> Nor doth he of himself know them for aught
> Till he behold them forméd in th' applause
> Where they're extended; who like an arch reverb'rate
> The voice again; or, like a gate of steel
> Fronting the sun, receives and renders back
> His figure and his heat. (III, 3: 115ff.)

This is an astonishing insight into envy. Envy says that we do
not know ourselves until we are applauded by others. Our own
voice is made clear to us only in the reverberations coming back

to us in others' applause. Then Ulysses uses a powerful image: the sun itself can know its shape and strength only where the steel gate gives "his figure and his heat" dazzlingly back to it.

In his book on Shakespeare, *A Theatre of Envy*, René Girard says that in *Troilus and Cressida* we see described a media-crazed world precisely like our own, a world wherein "the value of human beings is measured primarily by something we call their 'visibility'" (p. 145). To be visible is, in this sense, to be the object of every envious gaze. If the envious gaze of others is withdrawn—"if," says Girard, "the desires of these others are not riveted on him" (ibid.)—then he becomes invisible even to himself. In such a case, the person may well fall into a kind of self-hate, swept suddenly into a heartsick depression wherein (at least for a time) he cannot "see" himself as being himself.

The scene between Ulysses and Achilles where the speech occurs has further insights. The plot of the play, drawn from Homer, is surely familiar. Achilles, the greatest Greek warrior at the seige of Troy, has withdrawn from the fighting in envious anger at the Greek commander, Agamemnon, and consequently the Greeks begin to lose ground to the Trojans—such is the familiar starting point of the plot. Agamemnon calls together all his commanders (including, of course, Ulysses, the canniest strategist among the Greeks) to assess the situation. Shakespeare then invents a new plotline to fit perfectly his dramatization of envy in this play: he has Ulysses conceive a plan to deflect adulation away from Achilles and onto another (and far inferior) Greek warrior, Ajax. The point of Ulysses' plan is to make Achilles once more crave the envious gaze of others by depriving him of it, a craving that can be fed only—so Ulysses schemes—by Achilles returning to the battle and leading the Greeks to victory over Troy.

At least initially, the plan works precisely as Ulysses conceives it. In a stunning scene, he has the Greek commanders—all of whom have been, up to now, Achilles' envious admirers—deliberately snub Achilles with a finely dismissive contempt. And the very instant the adulation all at once ceases, Achilles becomes depressed. "What," he says to Ulysses, "are all my deeds forgot?" Shakespeare's point is plain: such strategic intelligence as Ulysses' resides solely in the capacity to read aright the dynamics of mimetic envy.

Then Ulysses responds to Achilles—and the speech is one of Shakespeare's masterpieces. Ulysses explains that in a world driven by envious resentments, no one and nothing can long hold any admiring gaze. For this is a world where, in Girard's words, "the pace of fashion accelerates; idols are erected and toppled at a faster and faster rate" (p. 148). Here are the first lines of Ulysses' great speech:

> Time hath, my Lord, a wallet at his back,
> Wherein he puts alms for oblivion,
> A great-sized monster of ingratitudes:
> Those scraps are good deeds past, which are devoured
> As fast as they are made, forgot as soon
> As done. (III, 3: 145ff.)

"This is an intensely historical world, a world where history is 'hot,'" says Girard (p. 148). Such heat is the direct result of envy's action, the intensities of which consume every good action of every good person the instant such actions occur. The present is therefore experienced as grounded in resentment, or ingratitude; it becomes the arena—or carnival—wherein we ceaselessly consume and instantly forget and endlessly crave again. In other words, the world of *Troilus and Cressida* is precisely our media-driven world of mimetic spins of desire.

At midpoint in his speech to Achilles, Ulysses says this:

> For time is like a fashionable host,
> That slightly shakes his parting guest by th' hand,
> And with his arms outstretched, as he would fly,
> Grasps in the comer: the welcome ever smiles,
> And farewell goes out sighing. (III, 3: 165ff.)

These lines, says Girard very perceptively, "make me think of the way popular hosts handle their guests on TV shows" (p. 148): the departing guest is quickly dismissed while the arriving one is grandly welcomed. A few lines later, Ulysses says that everything good and solid and true in the world—"beauty, wit, / High birth, vigor of bone, desert in service, / Love, friendship, charity"—"are subjects all / To envious and calumniating time" (ll. 171-74). This terrifying diagnosis of our spiritual sickness then reaches its dreadful conclusion: we have all—"with one consent" (l. 176)—become fatally infected with this relational disease called envy.

The drama of envy in *Troilus and Cressida* runs even wider and deeper. For the play's military situation is merely the framework within which the title characters conduct an erotic affair. This relationship, which occupies twelve of the play's twenty-one scenes, manifests the same dynamics of envy the war exhibits. Early in the play, Cressida observes that men sexually desire only women who arouse envy in other men, saying, "Men prize the thing ungained more than it is" (I, 2: 288). In Act IV, as their relationship is about to be rended by mimetic envy, Troilus responds to Cressida's question as to whether he really thinks that she will betray him by saying:

> No.
> But something may be done that we will not;
> And sometimes we are devils to ourselves,
> When we will tempt the frailty of our powers,
> Presuming on their changeful potency. (IV, 4: 92ff.)

Mimetic desire is in us a vastly stronger power than our will; and if we attempt to pit mere will against such desire, then we wind up becoming our own worst devils. Will power, says Troilus, is "changeful," its strength utterly unreliable against what he calls (a moment before) a "dumb-discoursive devil," i.e., one that communicates perfectly without speaking a single word. Troilus is here trying to teach Cressida how to *maneuver* in the teeth of mimetic desire, how to beat the demons of her own envious hungers. But the fate of the two lovers is exactly what happens in the battlefield to Achilles: violent rending. Thus, Shakespeare's point in connecting the love affair and the war is to show (in Girard's fine phrase) that all mimetic strategy "is nothing but a complicated form of self-delusion" (p. 149). Mimetic maneuvering only produces mimetic escalation and finally something like dismemberment: such is Shakespeare's diagnosis of the turmoil of envy.

At play's conclusion, Pandarus, who has steered and manipulated the mimetic process of the disastrous love affair, steps stage-front to speak an epilogue to us, the audience. In the closing couplet of the entire play, he tells us that he will die about two months hence of venereal disease, and that, *because we watched this play, we will be the direct heirs of his sickness.*

> Till then I'll sweat, and seek about for eases,
> And at that time bequeath you my diseases.
> (V, 10: 57-58)

Shakespeare's significance could not be plainer. Envy's effects are fatally contagious in the same way that sexual diseases are. Once infected, you can only "sweat" and try to ease the pain (presumably by maneuvering to win every mimetic competition). But, in this bleakest of Shakespeare's plays, you assuredly cannot be cured of the illness called envy. You can only infect everyone around you as you inevitably die of this relational disease.

The truth of envy lies in this: that somehow, mysteriously, the other does indeed possess what seems most deeply "ours"—our personhood. The lie of envy is that we must tear the other apart to get from him or her this precious treasure. Vladimir Lossky writes this:

> In short, we must decrease that the other may increase,
> and so we are most deeply fulfilled and become most
> truly ourselves.

It sometimes happens that a choral singer will sing under a conductor who accomplishes the relational miracle of loving *simultaneously* the whole choir and every individual singer in it. The simultaneity is the miracle—and the key. For by doing both forms of loving *at once*—loving each singer actively and tirelessly at the very same moment he is also loving every other singer—the conductor unmakes all mimetic desire. In this love, the conductor gives up every least shred of his own hunger for prestige in order to achieve one immense end: to give all his art entirely to his singers. He empties himself *of himself* so as to bestow upon every single singer the fullness of each singer's personhood in this music. This is a genuinely real experience. And it is an experience that marks the end of all mimetic envy.

A fine choral singer recently said of this experience, "When this happens, you feel like you're one of maybe two or three other singers—even when there's really two or three *hundred* others." Such love is best understood as *perfective:* for as it moves toward its own luminous perfection, it brings about perfection in others. Here, then, is *good* mimesis, for it is likely that the singers will follow their conductor's lead and give their art also to him.

Further, the experience of self-emptying love releases both conductor and choir from the always disintegrative search for the always illusory "ideal sound." Such a sound remains always maddeningly *just ahead* of any sound the choir is actually making; and therefore it is sound that neither conductor nor choir can ever actually achieve. Human sound detached from the concrete, embodied reality of any given human person, it is therefore detached from love. The pursuit of such chimerical sound is fueled in both singer and conductor by envy of its "ideal beauty" and resentment against the living choral reality. Here, then, is full-blown mimetic contagion. Its first fruits are despair and anger; later ones include indifference and contempt. Only the conductor's actively self-emptying love of her singers, each singly and all together—and from thence reciprocally between every singer—

can achieve any real release from these mimetic disintegrations.

In this way, choral conducting becomes a spiritual practice. And in being so, it can come to exhibit that spiritual reality wherein the conductor can begin through love to *quiet down* his own engagement in the mimetic turmoil all our lives exhibit. Such quieting down has long been known in the spiritual practices of Eastern Orthodox Christendom as the reality of stillness.

The single most essential book for any choral conductor is one that Russian novelist Fyodor Dostoevsky valued above every other book in the world, *The Ascetical Homilies of St. Isaac the Syrian.* Here is a passage from Homily 37, where St. Isaac first asks how we may know when a man has achieved stillness "in his manner of life," and then he answers:

> When a man is deemed worthy of constant prayer. . . .
> When the Spirit dwells in a man, as the Apostle says, he
> never ceases to pray, since the Spirit Himself always prays
> [within him]. Then, whether he sleeps or wakes, prayer is
> never separated from his soul. If he eats, or drinks, or lies
> down, or does something, or even in slumber, the sweet
> fragrances and perfumes of prayer effortlessly exhale in
> his heart. He does not possess prayer in a limited way,
> but even though it should be outwardly still, at every
> moment it ministers within him secretly. For the silence
> of the limpidly pure is called prayer by one of the Christ-
> bearers, because their thoughts are divine motions. The
> movements of a pure heart and mind are meek and gen-
> tle cries, whereby the pure chant in a hidden manner to
> the Hidden God. (p. 182)

This passage can be seen to respond interestingly to Ulysses' speech in Shakespeare. The huge Shakespearean mimetic "monster of ingratitude" devours all "good deeds" as "fast as they are made" because mimetic envy immediately swallows up in hatred what it seizes in admiration. In other words, nothing in mimetic envy abides, nothing holds, nothing stays still. In sharp contrast, St.

Isaac says that "constant prayer" in a man is never "separated from his soul," that its fragrances always "effortlessly exhale in his heart"—for that integrative gracefulness is what prayer's constancy means. Where the turmoil of envy is ceaselessly destabilizing one's psyche, or soul, constant prayer "at every moment" is stilling down one's soul by—a beautiful word—*ministering* within secretly. In his speech, Ulysses also says to Achilles, "The present eye praises the present object" (l. 180)—that is, the mimetic gaze is constantly drawn by the latest mimetic lure—and therefore "envious time" is always "calumniating time," at once outwardly vicious and inwardly vacuous. Constant prayer, on the other hand, makes all our inner processes into "divine motions," outwardly gentle and inwardly musical. Such prayer signals the reality of stillness in us.

When our life moves toward stillness, we begin to enter into a spiritual state that St. Isaac in his Homilies beautifully terms *limpid purity*. When this Isaacian term was translated from the original Syriac into Patristic Greek, *shapyutha* became *katharótes*, a Greek word that we know as *cathartic*. The point is clear: stillness *cleanses* us of every aspect of that relational affliction we call envy. The result, in St. Isaac, is a mental and emotional purification "whereby [we] chant in a hidden manner to the Hidden God." In a word, by achieving stillness and being thereby cleansed of all envy, we become *musicalized*: effortlessly and ceaselessly musicalized.

In Homily Four, St. Isaac says this:

> Consider yourself a stranger all the days of your life, wherever you may be, so that you may find deliverance from the injury which is born of familiarity. In every matter, consider yourself to be totally ignorant so as to escape the reproach which follows the suspicion that you wish to set aright other men's opinions. . . . If you begin to say something profitable, say it as though you yourself are still learning, and not with authority and shamelessness. (p. 33)

Understood as instructions to both the choral conductor and all her choral singers, this passage strikes at the source of every mimetic infection. By being the ill-at-ease stranger, one is freed of the arrogance that always elicits from others resentment and envy. When a conductor begins to speak to her chorus in such a way, she thereby frees both herself and her singers from what St. Isaac calls the "love of esteem, from which springs envy," and from the hunger for "human glory, which is the cause of resentment" (p. 15). The very course of the world is fueled by these passions of envy and resentment. Hence to make these passions in any way abate or cease in our relational lives is to bring the world's terrible "onward flow" (in his phrase) to a complete standstill. Then the sweetness of genuine stillness can begin in all our relations. And in such sweetness is all music grounded.

In the final scene of his late play *The Winter's Tale,* Shakespeare manifests what is perhaps his most miraculous insight. The situation in the play is this. In Act I, King Leontes becomes consumed with violent envy against his beloved wife, Hermione, and his dearest friend, Polixenes, for their supposed adultery. This charge of adultery is completely baseless; there is not even the slightest shred of evidence of anything even remotely amiss betwen Hermione and Polixenes; and there is every evidence that Leontes is simply—and violently—sick with the mimetic contagion of envy: and with *no cause* for the envy arising from the others whom he envies. Leontes' vicious accusation brings about his wife's death. And at the moment of her death, Leontes suddenly understands that she has been all along entirely innocent while he throughout has been dreadfully sick. With this understanding, Leontes then begins a penitential process under the direction of Paulina, his deceased wife's confidante and loyal friend.

In the play's final scene, when some sixteen years have passed in repentance, Leontes is led by Paulina to view a newly completed statue of his deceased wife. When Leontes sees the statue, he says this:

O, thus she stood,
Even with such life of majesty—warm life,
As now it coldly stands—when first I wooed her.
I am ashamed: does not the stone rebuke me,
For being more stone than it? (V, 3: 35ff.)

The years of Leontes' repentance are here focused in this terrible awareness: I am more stone than this statue. Such awareness
entirely reverses Leontes' earlier mode of relational life by turning
the pointing finger of his vicious accusation away from others (his
wife, his friend, and his loyal servants) and back toward his own
heart—and he does so in genuine humility. St. Isaac says, "The
man who endures accusations against himself with humility has
arrived at perfection, and he is marvelled at by the holy angels, for
there is no other virtue so great and so hard to achieve" (p. 43).
The repentance Leontes exhibits in this speech signals his
arrival—if not at perfection—at least at the point where his violent envy has genuinely abated. Such a point, Shakespeare says, is
where the real miracle of relational life can begin.

Then Paulina says, "If you can behold it, / I'll make the statue move indeed, descend /And take you by the hand" (ll. 87-89).
The relational miracle is about to strike: the miracle of resurrection. Paulina then speaks these extraordinary lines:

Music, awake her; strike.
'Tis time; descend; be stone no more; approach;
Strike all that look upon you with marvel; come;
I'll fill your grave up. Stir; nay, come away;
Bequeath to death your numbness; for from him
Dear life redeems you. (V, 3: 98ff.)

Hermione steps down from the pedestal, stone no more but fully
alive. Then it is revealed: she had not died sixteen years before but
had been hidden away by Paulina. And now, with Leontes fully
repentant, Hermione can stand forth again. From the passional
death accomplished through freely chosen repentance, Leontes'

real life has been resurrected. This moment of resurrection speaks back across a decade of Shakespeare's plays—a decade that includes *Othello, King Lear,* and *Macbeth*—to that terrible conclusion of *Troilus and Cressida* when we inherit the fatal mimetic and sexual contagion from Pandarus. Now we inherit the redemption of "Dear life."

Thus, with this (attractively improbable) tale of a statue coming to life, Shakespeare achieves his magnificent insight. In disengaging oneself from the dealing of mimetic violence to those one actually loves, one dies (as St. Isaac would say) to the whole "ongoing flow" of the envy-driven world. And in this dying, one begins truly to live.

Every choral conductor stands before his chorus in the way Leontes stands before the statue. In order for musical life truly to begin, something petrified in him, something like stone in him, must die in order for life to happen in his singers. The conductor's stony insensitivity is rooted in his mimetic contagion and is fed by the envy born of his hunger for prestige and the resentment arising from his exercise of power. And as the conductor can begin to awaken to his own heart's stoniness, he can begin to enter the miracle of stillness that all great music possesses. No technique in the world, either musical or spiritual, can bring the conductor even one inch toward that miracle. Only in fully, penitentially, and self-emptyingly loving the other—loving the singers and the composers, and above all loving the God who is Himself the fullness of every other love—can he begin to draw near the miracle. Every time he stands before his chorus, he inwardly says, "Music, awake us; strike." And it does.

In the Biblical narrative of the Garden and the Fall (Genesis 3), we see a situation wherein the serpent—as Girard's perceptive associate Gil Bailie explains—"tells Eve that the fruit will make her *like God,*" pointing out that even in circumstances "as unconducive to envy, covetousness, and resentment as the Garden of Eden, the serpent's gaudy desire is all that it takes to unhinge the human race and shove it on its grasping and violent 'career'" (p. 37). If the conductor is Leontes standing before the statue, then the choir resembles Eve in the Garden when the beguiling call into mimetic envy begins to sound. At such a moment (and it is almost every moment), the singer can either begin her "violent 'career'" of mimetic turmoil called musical prestige or she can choose the other path, the one wherein music can become that "constant prayer" called by St. Isaac *katharótes,* or *limpid purity.* On this path—opening in every choral moment, both rehearsal and performance—the singer *self-emptyingly gives all his art* to every other singer so that all of them—and *not* he, though he is included in the all—may be filled with the music's glory. Then the miracle occurs. Every other singer becomes, in voice and whole person, divinely and beautifully alive. And so does the music. And so does she.

Acknowledgments

The opening six paragraphs in this essay underwent some ten or so drafts, more than half composed by my wife, Carol Sheehan, university press editor and an Orthodox choir director. Without her beautiful work, this essay would not have happened. I am grateful, too, to Talia Darville and Rowan Sheehan of Westminster Choir College for their immense help in understanding the choral experience.

Bibliographical Note

Besides all of Shakespeare's plays as well as his Sonnets, the best presentation of mimetic theory is René Girard's book on Shakespeare, *A Theatre of Envy* (Oxford, 1991). Also useful is *The Girard Reader,* ed. James G. Williams (Crossroads, 1996), especially for its concluding interview with Girard—perhaps itself the best starting point to date for understanding Girard's theory. Gil Bailie's beautiful book, *Violence Unveiled* (Crossroads, 1995), is the clearest exposition of the Girardian discourse as an anthropology of violence. Vladimir Lossky's *Mystical Theology of the Eastern Church* (St. Vladimir's Seminary Press) offers, among much else, a profound Orthodox understanding of personhood. There is only one complete translation of *The Ascetical Homilies of St. Isaac the Syrian,* published by Holy Transfiguration Orthodox Monastery (Boston, 1984)—a magnificent edition with an excellent subject index.

Donald Sheehan teaches in English and Classics at Dartmouth College and directs The Robert Frost Place in Franconia, N.H. He is a Subdeacon in the Eastern Orthodox Church, the father of two grown sons, and lives with his wife in Sharon, Vermont. He is co-translator, with Olga Andrejev, of Fr. Pavel Florensky's Iconostasis (St. Vladimir's Seminary Press, 1996).

References and Further Reading
with Selected Annotations

Author's Note: Because of the divergent nature of the topic of this book, I wanted to provide some brief annotations concerning some of the books that shaped and helped my own thinking on this subject. Additionally, I hope to provide the reader with immediate further reading that will help you move and grow in understanding beyond the scope of this text.

Adams, Cass. ed. *The Soul Unearthed.* New York: Putnam Books, 1997.

Albom, Mitch. *Tuesdays with Morrie.* New York: Doubleday, 1997
This book, long on the best-seller lists, is a straightforward summary of some important life issues as seen from the eyes of a brave soul dying of Lou Gehrig's disease. Subject of the book was featured on *Nightline.*

Austin, James H. *Zen and the Brain.* Boston: Massachusetts Institute of Technology, 1998.
A massive and impressive book of scientific scholarship for those who want to delve into the scientific functioning of the soul through the mind.

Bacon, Francis. *Novum Organum (1620)* in C. Curtis and F. Greenslet, eds., *The Practical Cogitator.* Boston: Houghton-Mifflin, 1953.

Barks, Coleman, trans. *The Essential Rumi.* San Fransisco: Harper, 1995.

Barron, Frank, Alfonso Montuori, and Anthony Barron, eds. *Creators on Creating.* New York: Putnam Books, 1997.

Blum, David. *Casals and the Art of Interpretation.* Los Angeles: University of California Press, 1977.

Bonhoffer, Dietrich. *Life Together.* New York: Harper Collins, 1954.

Boulding, Maria, trans. *The Confessions of St. Augustine.* Hyde Park, NY: New City Press, 1997.
A beautiful translation of this classic work.

Brussat, Frederic and Mary Ann. *Spiritual Literacy.* New York: Scribner, 1996.

Bryan, Mark. *The Artist's Way at Work.* New York: William Morrow and Co., 1998.

Buechner, Frederick. *Wishful Thinking: A Seeker's ABC.* San Fransisco: Harper, 1993.

Buber, Martin. *I and Thou.* New York: Schribner, 1970.
Elaine Brown required this book for all her students. Highly recommended.

Buber, Martin. *Between Man and Man.* New York: Macmillian, 1965.

Buber, Martin. *The Prophetic Faith.* New York: Harper and Row, 1948.

Buber, Martin. *Two Types of Faith.* New York: Harper and Row Publishers, 1961.
This book describes issues of soulfulness as related to understanding what faith is.

Cameron, Julia. *The Artist's Way.* New York: G. Putman's Sons, 1992.
Since its publication, this book has pointed the way for many persons to understand the processes involved with becoming an artist.

Carrington, Patricia. *Learn to Meditate.* Boston: Element Books, 1998.

Crum, Thomas F. *Journey to Center: Lessons in Unifying Body, Mind, and Spirit.* New York: Fireside, 1997.

Csikszentmihalyi, Mihaly. *Creativity.* New York: HarperCollins Publishers, 1996.

De Alacantara, Pedro. *Indirect Procedures: A Musician's Guide to the Alexander Technique.* Oxford: Oxford University Press, 1997.

DeMello, Anthony. *Awareness: The Perils and Opportunities of Reality.* New York: Doubleday, 1990.
This book, written in a direct and simple style, discusses how important it is to be aware in order to learn about oneself and the world.

DeMello, Anthony. *Sadhana—A Way to God: Christian Exercises in Eastern Form.* New York: Doubleday, 1984.

Dostoevsky, Fyodor. *The Brothers Karamazov.* Translated and annotated by Richard Pevear and Larissa Volokhonsky. New York: Vintage Books, 1991.
Through this great work of literature, one can see and be taken through the mimetic issues of life. The book deserves attention from all musicians.

Eastman, Charles A. *The Soul of the Indian.* Lincoln: University of Nebraska Press, 1911. Current Reprint, 1980.

Ehrhart, W.D. *Vietnam-Perkasie.* Amherst: University of Massachusetts, 1995.
This remarkable book details a man's soulful journey through the hell of the Vietnam war, and then his life afterward as he returns home.

Eliade, Mircea. *The Nature of Religion: The Sacred and the Profane.* New York: Harcourt, Brace and Company, 1987.
One of the classic works in spirituality.

Epstein, Mark. *Going to Pieces without Falling Apart: A Buddhist Perspective on Wholeness—Lessons from Meditation and Psychotherapy.* New York: Broadway Books, 1998.

Floensky, Pavel. *Iconostasis.* Donald Sheehan, ed. Crestwood, NY: St. Vladimir's Seminary Press, 1996.

Fox, John. *Finding What You Didn't Lose: Expressing Your Truth and Creativity Through Poem Making*. New York: Putnam Books, 1995.

Frazer, J. G. *The Golden Bough*. New York: Macmillian, 1963.

Friedman, Maurice. *Martin Buber: The Life of Dialogue*. New York: Harper and Row, 1955.

Friedman, Maurice, ed. *Pointing the Way: Martin Buber*. New York: Harper and Row, 1957.

Galache, Gabriel. *Praying Body and Soul: Methods and Practices of Anthony DeMello*. New York: The Crossroad Publishing Company, 1997.

Gelb, Michael J. *How to Think Like Leonardo Da Vinci*. New York: Delacorte Press, 1998.

Gomes, Peter J. *Sermons: Biblical Wisdom for Daily Living*. New York: William Morrow and Company, 1998.
Books by Peter Gomes, including this one, help to clarify issues in religion and its relationship to faith. His style of writing is direct, honest, and very inspirational.

Heschel, Abraham Joshua. *God in Search of Man*. New York: The Noon Day Press, 1955.

Heschel, Abraham Joshua. *Who Is Man?* Stanford: Stanford University Press, 1965.
All the books by Rabbi Heschel provide profound insights into what it is to be human. Musicians should take time to read his works.

Hillman, James. *Kinds of Power: A Guide to Its Intelligent Uses*. New York: Doubleday, 1995.

Hillman, James. *The Soul's Code: In Search of Character and Calling*. New York: Random House, 1996.

Hillman, James. *The Thought of the Heart and the Soul of the World*. Woodstock, CT: 1981.
James Hillman is one of the twentieth century's greatest psychologists. His

writings constantly explore the nature of the soul and its relationship to the psychological life of each of us. These books would provide much material for thought for musicians.

Holy Transfiguration Monastery, trans. *The Ascetical Homilies of Saint Issac the Syrian.* Boston: Holy Transfiguration Monastery, 1984.
This massive book contains a lifetime of reading concerning lessons on simplicity, humbleness, loving, and finding one's soulfulness. A unique and profound book.

Lambert, Craig. *Mind Over Water: Lessons on Life from the Art of Rowing.* New York: Houghton Mifflin, 1998.

Levoy, Gregg. *Callings: Finding and Following an Authentic Life.* New York: Harmony Books, 1997.
This book should be required reading for all artists. It brings remarkable clarity to the subject of approaching one's calling in life. The author describes why people avoid callings and how they can help themselves to follow their destinies while maintaining their souls.

Marty, Martin E. *A Cry of Absence: Reflections from the Winter of The Heart.* Grand Rapids, Michigan: William E. Eerdmans Publishing Company, 1997.

Marty, Martin and Michah Marty. *When True Simplicity Is Gained: Finding Spirituality in a Complex World.* Grand Rapids, Michigan: William B. Eerdmanns Publishing Company, 1998.

McElroy, Susan Chernak. *Animals As Guides for the Soul.* New York: Ballantine, 1998.

McNiff, Shaun. *Art As Medicine.* Boston: Shambhala, 1992.

Meyers, Diana Tietjens. *Feminists Rethink the Self.* New York: HarperCollins Publishers, 1997.

Moore, Thomas. ed. *The Education of the Heart.* New York: Harper Perennial, 1996.

Murdoch, Iris. *The Sovereignty of Good.* London: Routledge, 1970.

Naht Hanh, Thich. *Peace Is Every Step: The Path of Mindfulness in Everyday Life.* New York: Bantam Books, 1991.
A profound book presenting simple wisdom for the care of one's soul.

Nietzsche, Friedrich. *Human, All Too Human.* Lincoln: University of Nebraska Press, 1984.

Palmer, Parker J. *The Active Life: Wisdom for Work, Creativity, and Caring.* San Fransisco: Harper, 1990.

Palmer, Parker J. *The Courage to Teach: Exploring the Inner Landscape of a Teacher's Life.* San Fransisco: Jossey-Bass Publishers, 1998.
One of the most influential books the author has read on the subject of teaching and its relationship to soulfulness. The book is not only informative, but truly inspirational. It should be required reading for all musician/teachers.

Palmer, Parker J. *To Know As We Are Known: Education As a Spiritual Journey.* San Fransisco: Harper, 1993.

Ramachandran, V. S. and Sandra Blakeslee. *Phantoms in the Brain.* New York: William Morrow and Company, 1998.

Rank, Otto. *Psychology and the Soul: A Study of the Origin, Conceptual Origin and Nature of the Soul.* Baltimore: The Johns Hopkins University Press, 1998 (new edition).

Richards, M. C. *Centering: In Pottery, Poetry, and the Person.* Second Edition. Middletown, CT: Wesleyan University Press, 1989.
This classic book describes centering through the analogy of being a potter. This book was also required reading for students of Elaine Brown

Rothenberg, Albert. *Creativity and Madness.* Baltimore: The Johns Hopkins University Press, 1990.

Rothschild, Fritz A. ed. *Between God and Man: An Interpretation of Judaism from the Writings of Abraham J. Heschel.* London: Free Press Paperbacks, 1959.

Shaku, Soyen. *The Practice of Dhyanna.* In *The Anthology of Zen.* W. Briggs. New York: L. Grove Press.

Skees, Suzanne. *God Among the Shakers: A Search for Stillness and by Faith at Sabbathday Lake.* New York: Hyperion, 1998.

Smith, Robert Lawrence. *A Quaker Book of Wisdom.* New York: William Morrow and Company, 1998.

Stanislavski, Constantin. *An Actor Prepares.* New York: Routledge, 1964.

Sternberg, Robert J. *The Nature of Creativity.* Cambridge: Cambridge University Press, 1988.

Taylor, Charles. *Sources of Self.* Cambridge: Harvard University Press, 1989.

Thoreau, Henry David. *Walden, 1854.* Princeton: Princeton University Press, 1989.

Tillich, Paul. *The Courage to Be.* New Haven: Yale University Press, 1952.

Trungpa, Chögyam. *Cutting Through Spiritual Materialism.* Boston and London: Shambhala Publications, 1973.

Vasileios, Archmandrite. *Abba Issac the Syrian: An Approach to His World.* Montreal, Canada: Alexander Press, 1997.

Waskow, Arthur. *Godwrestling—Round 2: Ancient Wisdom, Future Paths.* Woodstock, CT: Jewish Lights Publishing, 1996.

White, Perry D. *The Whole Conductor: Weston Noble's Philosophies on the Psychology of Conducting and Musicianship.* DMA Dissertation. Norman, Oklahoma: The University of Oklahoma, 1998.
This new dissertation details the spiritual journey of one of America's most respected and loved choral conductors.

Williams, James G. *The Girard Reader.* New York: The Crossroad
    Publishing Company, 1996.
    For those who wish to do further reading on mimetics, this is a primary
    source of information concerning mimetic theory as espoused by Rene
    Girard.

Zaleski, Philip. *Spiritual Writing.* San Fransisco: Harper, 1998.

Zukav, Gary. *The Seat of the Soul.* New York: Simon and Schuster,
    1990.

Index of
Quoted Persons

About the Author

One of America's most respected choral conductors and educators, James Jordan is associate professor of conducting at Westminster Choir College of Rider University, a leading center for the study and performance of choral music, where he is conductor of the Westminster Chapel Choir.

Dr. Jordan's unique educational background in conducting, the psychology of music, dance education, and psychology allow him to make poignant observations into the music-making process from the vantagepoint of a conductor.

An internationally recognized pedagogue, his theories of rhythm pedagogy and movement are now widely applied in music education for the teaching of rhythm to children and adults. His four textbooks and several videos on the subjects of Group Vocal Technique, Ensemble Diction, and Conducting are used for the education of teachers and conductors around the world. His conducting text, *Evoking Sound* was his first book with GIA Publications.

Prior to his appointment to the distinguished Westminster faculty, he served as chair for music education at the Hartt School of Music. He has also held positions at the School of the Hartford Ballet and the Pennsylvania State University. He holds degrees from Susquehanna University (BM) and Temple University (MM and Ph.D.) His study in the psychology of music has been with Edwin E. Gordon. His conducting teachers have been Elaine Brown, Wilhelm Ehmann, Volker Hempfling and Gail B. Poch.